ISD
From the Ground Up

A No-Nonsense Approach to Instructional Design

D1293713

Chuck Hodell

If no CD-ROM is included with this book, please go to
www.astd.org/ISDFromtheGroundUp
to download all handouts and other materials to your hard drive.

Alexandria, VA

ASTD Press is an internationally renowned source of insightful and practical information on workplace learning and performance topics, including training basics, evaluation and return-on-investment (ROI), instructional systems development (ISD), e-learning, leadership, and career development.

Ordering information: Books published by ASTD Press can be purchased by visiting our website at store.astd.org or by calling 800.628.2783 or 703.683.8100.

Library of Congress Control Number: 2006931279

ISBN-10: 1-56286-455-6
ISBN-13: 978-1-56286-455-2

Director: Cat Russo
Manager, Acquisitions & Author Development Editor: Mark Morrow
Editorial Manager: Jacqueline Edlund-Braun
Copyeditor: Karen Eddleman
Indexer: April Davis
Interior Design and Production: Kathleen Schaner
Cover Design: Renita Wade
Cover Illustration: John S. Dykes

Contents

Preface

Need for an ISD Book for Students and Practitioners

The field of instructional design is a dynamic enterprise with numerous perspectives, approaches, and philosophies concerning every aspect of the topic. Whether one considers constructivist or behaviorist theory to be more persuasive, or whether objectives need to be observable and measurable or would be perfectly acceptable at the "understanding" level of sophistication, the topic of instructional design often starts a healthy debate.

As a student, practitioner, and teacher in the field of instructional systems development (ISD), I have found that most of the information available for both prospective and practicing instructional designers is either too elementary or overly theoretical. It seemed to me that a practical guide to meet the needs of both populations would allow a solid base of practical knowledge and a set of skills that would address most design scenarios.

My beliefs center squarely on the notion that instructional design is a system that is dynamic enough to address almost all challenges that trainers and educators encounter in the course of their instructional design careers. The particulars of any instructional design process, such as content, instructional methods, and so forth, are individual elements that will probably always be different from one project to another. What remains constant is the ISD process that drives important decisions relating to content, instructional methods, and materials. A seasoned instructional designer weighs each separate element of a project and provides a range of solutions for specific needs. There is no one-size-fits-all approach to ISD; no single solution would work in the vast majority of cases. Each project requires a specially tailored ISD process.

If a reader takes anything from this book, I hope it is this: Instructional design is a system that is dynamic enough to work with any set of variables regardless of the particulars. Just as any new building project demands a blueprint to be successful, any instructional design endeavor needs ISD to be successful. And, because every blueprint is different, every instructional design is different, varying only in detail but never in purpose.

Why a Second Edition?

Since the first edition of this book was published in 2000, many readers have asked that I include instructional design tools for more advanced designers. These needs were most often expressed by people involved in programs that use this book as a text in their master's level ISD and education programs and courses. It is in that light that this second edition was written, and I hope the new chapters and the accompanying CD containing information and tools relating to criticality, quality ratings, and accreditation serve a wider ISD audience of students and practitioners.

Acknowledgments

I wish to express my special appreciation to Dr. J. Marvin Cook, the man who patiently taught me ISD and shared his years of experience with me and all his students; to all of my colleagues in the administration and faculty of the National Labor College, including President Susan Schurman, Provost Pat Greenfield, and the members of the Educational Design Unit past and present including Jean Dearden, Julie Mendez-de Leon, Rob Morriss, Cindy Cooke, Christa Dicky, Isaac Wilson, Nalini Roy, Lydia Clemons, and Patricia Yeghissian; to all my sisters and brothers in the labor movement; to all those teaching in labor education and apprenticeship; to my colleagues at the University of Maryland Baltimore County (UMBC), including Greg Williams, Ginny Story, Adriana Val, Jodi Crandall, Ana Maria Schwartz, John Nelson, Tom Field, Diane Lee, Zane Berge, and Marie de Verneil; to my graduate students at UMBC who assisted me with the first edition of this book including Dawn Kane, Vicky Passion Graff, Amy Rossmark, Bernadette Fortenbaugh, Brian J. Reider, Charlotte Leer, Ginger Butcher, and Dana Michelle Karp; and to all of my students, past and present.

Dedication

In memory of my father, Tex Hodell, who passed away during the writing of this second edition; to my children, Heather, David, and Joe; and to Carol D'Agostino for her tireless support.

Chuck Hodell
August 2006

Introduction

Handbook and Mentor for Instructional Designers

The practice of instructional systems development (ISD) is often such a diverse and seemingly transparent enterprise that many practitioners fail to recognize their role as an instructional designer. They think of themselves as teachers, facilitators, trainers, managers, academics, or thousands of other occupations that include responsibility for designing or delivering training or education. And, of course, there are the countless millions who stand in front of an audience and make presentations at gatherings ranging in size from small meetings to large conventions or seminars.

Every instructional designer has started in the same place in this field—at the beginning. Some learn experientially through trial and error, often consulting a book or website for ideas, whereas others have the advantage of being mentored by a veteran designer. This book, along with the companion CD, offers the benefits of

Where Are All the Instructional Designers?

Millions of instructional designers exist. They can be found in any location where a teacher stands in front of a classroom, an apprenticeship instructor teaches workers a skilled trade, a trainer gathers a group in the company conference room for an orientation session, or a volunteer works with an underserved population in a small meeting room in a village or hamlet in some corner of the world. Instructional designers are everywhere, and they are seldom recognized for their contributions or given any tangible support in their efforts. This is one reason this book was originally written and, now in its second edition, strives to provide every designer a handbook of skills to refer to or learn from according to his or her needs.

1

a handbook and a mentor and makes them each readily available, perhaps next to your computer or in your briefcase.

This book provides both novice and experienced instructional designers a series of tools to reference as they practice their profession. Included are such basics as the ADDIE (analyze, design, development, implementation, and evaluation) model of ISD, analysis tools, tips on how to write objectives, and the two essential deliverables in ISD—the design plan and the lesson plan.

For designers seeking advanced tools, this edition includes several new chapters that include the introduction of quality control instruments for objectives, design plans, and lesson plans. Included is a methodology for making tough content decisions by determining which content is essential by applying a concept called criticality. Additionally, there is a section on designing courses for college credit. All in all, there is something for every level of instructional design experience.

Designer's Handbook

This book gives you the chance to practice ISD skills as you read. Exercises relating to the topic of each individual chapter are contained on the accompanying CD and give you a chance to practice assembling components of a design plan and a lesson plan. A design plan is the blueprint for a training project and includes all the basic elements of instructional design, including behavioral objectives, evaluation tasks, prerequisites for both learners and facilitators, and other essential components you will be introduced to later in the book. The lesson plan is the delivery system that takes the design plan and presents it to the end user of the training, the learner.

The essential ISD skills you will learn or review include the following:

- analyzing systems, both general and instructional
- defining and working with the generic ADDIE model of instructional design
- performing various analysis operations including population and task analysis and designing and implementing focus group sessions
- writing objectives and evaluation tasks, and performing other design-phase tasks
- constructing design plans and lesson plans
- performing skills related to the development phase including pilot testing and materials development
- implementing designers' tools
- writing and implementing various evaluation strategies, including Kirkpatrick's (1998) four levels of evaluation
- using skills related to web-based training.

The advanced skills you will have at your fingertips include

- quality rating for objectives (QRO)
- quality rating for design plans (QRDP)
- quality rating for lesson plans (QRLP)
- the criticality matrix
- designing for credit.

Instructional design isn't any more difficult to learn and put to use than any other professional process. However, a gap exists between the great and the marginal designs in the real world. There are as many different ways to design a new-employee orientation as there are new employees, but few actually make a new employee feel as if he or she made the right decision in picking a new employer. The difference between a great orientation and a marginal orientation is often in the use of ISD to design training. The use of a system to design and implement the program pays dividends in the way training "feels" to the participants and the benefits it offers an organization.

ISD is a systems approach to training. You may hear it called instructional development, instructional systems design, systems approach to training, or several other terms. They all refer to similar approaches to designing curriculum. You will find while working your way through this book that ISD is often nothing more than common sense with a plan. Sometimes it just takes someone to point out the relationship between different aspects of instructional design and offer methodologies and shortcuts to make the process more efficient. What commonly defines a professional is the ability to make something look easy. After learning and practicing the basics of ISD, you will be moving toward becoming a professional instructional designer.

Though it may look easy to the uninitiated, ISD is a complex set of skills that must be mastered. From the outside it appears that designing a curriculum is a straightforward process, but below the surface a number of design skills and processes combine to form a project of mythic proportions. New-employee orientation becomes the organizational equivalent to the pyramids—something that stands the test of time.

What Skills Are Required?

A number of specialized skills must be present in an instructional designer's tool kit. The designer's tool kit consists of a variety of both basic and advanced instructional design tools for use one at a time or in combination to form a battery of skills to address one or a hundred design challenges.

Read through the list of instructional design skills in table I-1, and determine if you have each skill. This is not a test. It only serves as a snapshot of where you begin the process of building your tool kit. For right now, check "yes" or "no" to the questions posed in the table. Later, you will have an opportunity to compare your beginning skills with your ending skills.

Building Your Design Skills

Readers have the luxury of using this book several ways, depending on their needs. Whether working on a design project or brushing up on a specific aspect of instructional design, readers can consult the chapters that fit their needs. If they are just starting out in the field and are not working on a specific project, they can get an in-depth look at the steps in an instructional project.

The book follows one instructional design project—construction of a poison prevention course—from start to finish so readers can see how it is done. That project appears in the exercises that are on the CD. The subject matter is not intended for actual implementation but to illustrate the instructional design process. After reading each description of the poison prevention project, readers may return to it, substituting a project they are working on or any other subject matter they choose. The poison prevention material is intended to serve as a placeholder for readers' own content.

Table I-1. Skills inventory.

Do You Know How to...	Yes	No
Conduct a population analysis?	☐	☐
Design and implement a focus group session?	☐	☐
Write four-part objectives?	☐	☐
Name the four objective domains?	☐	☐
Define and provide examples of at least three instructional methods?	☐	☐
Define and provide examples of at least three distribution methods?	☐	☐
Write at least two evaluation tasks?	☐	☐
Explain the performance agreement principle using an example?	☐	☐
Design evaluations for each of the four Kirkpatrick levels?	☐	☐
Complete a design plan?	☐	☐
Construct a lesson plan?	☐	☐

Readers also have the option of using the design plan (discussed in chapter 8) and the lesson plan (discussed in chapter 9) and the completed Lesson Plan for Poison Prevention in the Home—all contained on the companion CD—as templates for their own projects. They have the luxury of picking and choosing the elements of each chapter that fit their needs.

Who Needs This Book?

This book is a practitioner's guide to ISD and is grounded more in reality than scores of other textbooks are. Readers who are still building their ISD skills will find this book a useful and practical guide, without a great deal of academic theory. Advanced practitioners will find it an excellent in-service resource for reviewing their skills and then adding new skills to an already impressive resume of ISD knowledge and practice.

Both groups of readers will find that this book and the CD provide the basics of great instructional practice as well as practical ways to apply the principles. The CD contains all the exercises that enable readers to gain experience applying the ISD concepts. As they work through each exercise, readers will gain confidence in their use of the concept and find ways to put them to work.

The book is useful for designers at any level of experience or working in any design environment, including small or large organizations, nonprofits or corporations, and schools or training centers. One of the biggest myths about instructional design is that it is really only useful when integrated in a large organization. Nothing could be further from the truth. In fact, the largest gains in efficiency and participant success are often in environments that are either strapped for resources, such as nonprofits and community groups, or in one-person operations, such as classroom teachers or small training organizations. This is true for several reasons, not the least of which is that even incremental moves toward efficiency in small organizations reap great advantages.

Another advantage of this book is that it allows a designer to review previous work and gauge where projects might be improved or updated. No course is ever more than 90 percent complete if you work from the premise that every project can be improved. Review is an essential part of all instructional design, no matter how well done, even a design that is completed using this book as a guide. As with any creative process, time may change one's perspective. The design that seemed perfect two days before may suddenly appear seriously flawed. This is one advantage of a systems approach to instructional design, given that evaluation is essential to the design process. Committing even a short time to evaluation will yield improvements when it is conducted with an objective eye. It is the ISD equivalent of counting to 10 when someone's upset and wants to speak his or her mind. Evaluation provides time for reflection and reconsideration.

Accumulation of Advantages

If you play chess, you have probably heard the term *accumulation of advantages.* To a chess master, it means that a player has to complete a number of individual steps correctly to win a match. Most great chess players are thinking many moves ahead to chart out a strategy and prepare a defense to counter any move an opponent might make.

In ISD, accumulation of advantages is about making sure a designer makes all the right moves when designing curriculum. For example, it is impossible to have a great project if a designer leaves out analysis or evaluation. A designer needs to be three steps ahead of any problems in implementing a project and providing solutions when they do arise. For the chess player or the instructional designer, accumulation of advantages is a concept that means winning, and a designer always wants a winning project.

How This Book Is Arranged

This book is presented with a practitioner's eye toward instructional design, not as an academic look at the subject. Although there are many excellent publications that cover theoretical issues associated with ISD, rank-and-file instructional designers generally appreciate a just-in-time approach to ISD that includes readily implementable tools and processes.

This book contains five sections designed to help readers build or enhance their skills as instructional designers. Generally, readers will find the basics in sections 1 and 2, practice in section 3, advanced designer skills in section 4, and additional skills-enhancement materials in section 5. Following is an overview of what readers will find in each section:

- Section 1, "The Basics of ISD," contains the essentials of ISD. It sets the foundation for the remainder of readers' travels through the book as they visit systems and learn why an instructional system is integral to success as an instructional designer. The poison prevention project begins here.
- Section 2, "Working Through the ADDIE Model," is the nucleus of ISD as readers explore analysis, design, development, implementation, and evaluation in greater detail. They will explore various designer tools, including focus groups, writing objectives, designing evaluation instruments, and many other important aspects of ISD.
- Section 3, "The Basics of the Design and Lesson Plans," provides readers with both a design plan and lesson plan, which serve as learning tools and job aids. Readers can use these tools to assemble their own projects or just

use the model as a point of reference. The poison prevention project takes final form here.

- ■ Section 4, "The Quality Rating Process and Tools," allows the more advanced instructional designer a chance to drill deeper into three key ISD areas: objectives, design plans, and lesson plans. Readers can also find strategies for making tough content decisions using a criticality matrix. Finally, the notion of designing a course with the option of seeking college credit worthiness for the course is discussed.
- ■ Section 5, "Tips for Success," covers skills enhancement and looks to the future.

The chapters in each section relate to specific themes in instructional design. The arrangement of each topic allows readers to analyze their needs quickly in a specific design area and move where they need to be.

In addition to the exercises that will help readers apply the concepts in each chapter, the accompanying CD includes a completed lesson plan for the poison prevention course, Poison Prevention in the Home. It also includes a list of additional resources to guide readers who want to know more about ISD, including practical applications and theory.

Learn and enjoy!

Section 1 The Basics of ISD

1 Instructional Systems and the ADDIE Model

Chapter Objectives

At the conclusion of this chapter, you should be able to

- define an instructional system
- define the ADDIE model of ISD
- list advantages and disadvantages of instructional systems.

Instructional Systems

From the perspective of an instructional designer, any undertaking that includes a learner and the subject matter necessary to learn requires an instructional system. Instructional designers need inputs (subject matter and resources), a process (ISD), and outputs (curriculum and materials) to build a training course. This combination of elements is called an instructional system. (See the sidebar for a list of key definitions.)

This book describes an instructional system that has at its core five elements: analysis, design, development, implementation, and evaluation. This model is commonly referred to as the ADDIE model, after the first letter of each word.

Systems in Instructional Design

The term *systems analysis* has been used in countless contexts to reflect the process of analyzing the various elements of a system and determining the interaction of

Key Definitions

- An *instructional system* is an organized and arranged collection of instructional resources that, when combined, achieves the goal of addressing and providing appropriate training solutions.
- An *extended instructional system* comprises all elements external to the instructional system that have the potential to affect the design process.
- A *project* is a single design effort using an instructional system's approach. The three forms of projects are as follows:
  — *Singular:* one designer working alone to complete a project
  — *Multiple:* more than one designer usually operating within a single departmental or organizational unit
  — *Matrixed:* a combination of designers working with other organizational units.

each system element to other same-system elements and interaction of all related individual systems to each other. System analysis can prove to be a very intricate undertaking depending on the complexity of each system and elements. In ISD, the focus is on the elements and systems that influence course design and development, specifically from the perspective of the designer and the requirements for a sound instructional design process and product.

Like any system analysis, in ISD the instructional designer is looking for ways to make better decisions and thereby create better course and program designs than would have resulted without taking the design process to this level of sophistication. Thorough analysis of all the elements in a specific training or education system provides a designer the foundation for the traditional design process of producing course materials, lesson plans, and so forth. It is the very heart of the design plan process.

System-speak also includes terms such as *policy analysis, cost-benefit analysis, feasibility analysis,* and *consequence analysis.* These are all subsets of the process and are important to review if you are going to become firmly rooted in the systems process. For this book, the focus is on the systems related specifically to instructional design that are embodied in the ADDIE model of ISD.

ADDIE Model

The ADDIE model or some derivative of it provides designers with the necessary structure for designing any curriculum, regardless of the instructional methods employed. Anything from classroom lecture to distance learning starts and ends with the same fundamentals—the ADDIE model.

In the ADDIE model, analysis is the input for the system; design, development, and evaluation are the processes; and implementation is the output. These elements overlap somewhat, depending on the project, and because the system is dynamic, there will be some sharing of duties. This book examines in depth each of the five elements of the ADDIE model, which are described briefly in the following sections.

Analysis

Analysis is the data-gathering element of instructional design. Here, instructional designers assemble all the information they can possibly gather about the project before they consider anything else. Decisions about every aspect of the project must eventually be made. The information that instructional designers gather at this stage will be put to use throughout the system, so it is necessary that they have every scrap of data to ensure the design will be successful.

Design

Design is the blueprinting stage of instructional systems during which instructional designers create the blueprint for a project with all the specifications necessary to complete the project. During this stage, instructional designers write the objectives, construct course content, and complete the design plan.

Development

Materials production and pilot testing are the hallmarks of *development.* At this stage, most nondesigners begin to see progress. Everything from lecture notes to virtual reality is brought from design to deliverable.

Before instructional designers move from development to implementation, it is wise for them to do pilot testing to ensure that deliverables do not have to be redeveloped. Because of the time and expense involved, no one wants to reprint manuals or recode a technology-based project after a project goes into implementation. The pilot testing process allows organizations to implement any necessary changes in the project before the expenses associated with materials development are realized. The time and effort expended in pilot testing are well worth the effort, for this reason alone. Pilot testing also helps designers feel confident that what they have designed works.

Implementation

The most familiar of the elements is *implementation.* At implementation, the design plan meets the learner, and the content is delivered. The evaluation process that most designers and learners are familiar with takes place in this element. Evaluation is used to gauge the degree to which learners meet objectives and facilitators or technologies deliver the project.

Evaluation

Evaluation doesn't deserve to be listed last in the ADDIE model because it takes place in every element and surrounds the instructional design process. Evaluation is a constant guard at the gate of failure.

The advantages of using an instructional system are numerous, the most important being the ability to design projects quickly and efficiently. Nothing is left to chance or ignored when a designer stays within the framework of the ADDIE or other ISD models. One possible disadvantage is the necessity of a designer to be familiar with the ISD process.

The ADDIE Model at Work

To frame the ADDIE model in operational terms, it is useful to view the various key steps in each phase as viewed from an instructional designer's perspective.

Analysis

1. Frame the challenge, problem, or need into tangible action items.
2. Determine if each is an instructional or noninstructional issue.
3. Forward noninstructional items to appropriate resources for resolution.
4. Evolve strategies for instructional issues.
5. Gather data.
6. Determine needed resources.
7. Draft a budget and timeline.
8. Obtain sign-off from manager or client (if appropriate).
9. Evaluate all analysis elements.

Design

1. Draft a design plan as your blueprint for the project:
   - Rationale
   - Objectives
   - Population profile
   - Course description
   - Learner and facilitator prerequisites
   - Evaluation strategy
   - Deliverables.
2. Evaluate all design elements.

Development

1. Draft the lesson plan:
   - Gaining attention
   - Direction
   - Recall

- Content
- Application feedback—level 1
- Application feedback—level 2
- Application feedback—level 3
- Evaluation
- Closure.
2. Draft the materials (where applicable).
3. Draft online content (where applicable).
4. Pilot test (as applicable).
5. Modify as necessary based on pilot testing evaluation.
6. Evaluate all development elements.

Implementation

1. Move project to active status.
2. Evaluate (Kirkpatrick levels 1–3):
   - Reaction
   - Learning
   - Behavior.
3. Modify as necessary based on evaluation.
4. Evaluate all implementation elements.

Evaluation

1. Review all five ADDIE elements continuously.
2. Revise evaluation process as necessary.

An ADDIE Model Real-World Example

A description of the way an employee at one company applied the ADDIE model follows. The company, which requested anonymity, provides information technology to manage food and beverage operations at ballparks, stadiums, arenas, casinos, and other establishments in the hospitality industry. Brian Reider, the instructional designer, was considering creating a course for installers, support technicians, dealer representatives, and hardware technicians. The course would provide these staff members with the information they needed to provide the best possible customer support.

Below are the steps Reider followed as he applied the ADDIE model to creation of a course.

Problem

Reider defined the immediate institutional problem as whether to create a training course as a way to allow the company to continue providing the best support for the customer. One consideration he noted was that he was not an expert on hardware.

Analysis

During this data-gathering stage, Reider tried to get answers to these questions:

- Why do we need this course?
- What makes this hardware so different from the other that it needs its own course?
- What information needs to be covered in the course?

He used face-to-face interviews to gather information that would be relevant in the course. He interviewed support technicians (software and hardware), installation technicians, hardware technical writers, members of the hardware research and development department, and the director of hardware services to establish what information is necessary for a technician in the field. He also read support cases to see what some of the major problem areas were.

He concluded that the following topics should be included in the course:

- how this software and hardware are different from others
- basic knowledge of all components (parts identification)
- what parts are replaceable
- how to install the replacement parts
- how to convert one model to the newer model
- how to use some basic troubleshooting techniques.

Design

In this blueprinting stage of instructional design, Reider created observable and measurable terminal objectives for the course. The design took into account the need to integrate evaluation later in the development. Reider had subject matter experts (SMEs) review the objectives and provide feedback.

From the objectives, he determined that the best delivery method for instruction would be an instructor-led course with extensive hands-on exercises. He created an organizational chart (similar to a course or topic map) so that he had a graphical representation of the topics and subtopics to be discussed. This helped him group and link different topics to one another. It also allowed him to create the necessary enabling objectives.

Development

Producing materials and pilot testing are the main elements of this stage. For developing the course, Reider followed the nine events of instruction, which Gagne, Briggs, and Wager (1988) developed as a sequence for lesson plan design. (A description of the nine events of instruction appears in chapter 4.) Reider also maintained contact with some SMEs to ensure that the material he was creating was accurate.

Reider was becoming more knowledgeable about the hardware and was actually able to identify, remove, and replace all of the replaceable parts. While it was disassembled, he and other staff members used a digital camera to photograph the different components. They used these photographs for a parts identification job aid on the company's website.

Reider did not create a formal evaluation for the course due to the constraints on the length of the course and the purpose of the course.

Implementation

The course was implemented soon thereafter.

Evaluation

Before formal implementation of the course, a pilot class was held. The participants in the pilot class were new hires and members of the training department. The participants had no knowledge of the hardware. At the end of the pilot class, Reider convened a focus group to obtain feedback on the course. The participants completed a level 1 evaluation (reaction) form. Revision to the course was made on the basis of responses from the focus group, responses on a level 1 course evaluation, and the feedback from the instructor.

Reider reported that he made a few changes based on the level 1 evaluation and the focus group responses. The course received great reviews, and the students enjoyed the hands-on activity. Reider taught the course at various company offices throughout the United States as well as to company employees in Germany and Hong Kong.

Other ISD Models

There are probably as many informal ISD models as there are instructional designers, and that is the way it should be with ISD. Although many formal models exist for instructional designers to follow and learn from, each individual designer does things a little bit differently in the real world. No two projects evolve exactly the same way, and there have never been two instructional designers designing projects the same way. In fact, not every instructional designer uses the ADDIE model, but its five elements—analysis, design, development, implementation, and evaluation—should always be operational in instructional design.

As an instructional designer gains experience, the ISD elements combine in a way that works uniquely for him or her. Derivations of any model are necessary to meet different design strategies. Different designers write objectives differently, and no two surveys ever look exactly the same. Every designer eventually evolves to create a unique model of ISD based on the same fundamental ADDIE structure. It is not uncommon in some ISD models to see an additional level of analysis or evaluation or another element added to meet a specific design or organizational need. That it is why it is safe to say there are as many ISD models as there are instructional designers.

The cardinal rule of ISD is to never leave out analysis and evaluation, the two most commonly overlooked and abused elements of the model. Projects without analysis and evaluation can be spotted quickly because (1) they seldom work and (2) no one ever really figures out why they failed.

In Conclusion

The saying that hard work is usually disguised as luck resonates in training. The most successful training programs have the appearance of being effortlessly designed and delivered. The content is appropriate for the audience, there is just enough material to cover the time allowed, participants are able to meet the objectives, and evaluations ensure that the course design provides the desired results.

At the other extreme, a program that was put together with little planning or little thought about the desired results leaves learners confused, and the evaluations, if there are any, concentrate on nontraining issues like the comfort of the chairs or the cleanliness of the restrooms. Participants leave those programs wondering why they bothered to invest their time. The difference between these two situations typically is directly related to the time and expertise invested in the instructional design process. The evidence that a program has been well designed can be observed in the participants: They have learned.

Putting What You Have Learned Into Action

Now, let's work through some exercises to build your confidence and start you on the road to designing a course of your own. You will find exercises 1-1, 1-2, and 1-3 on the accompanying CD. Exercise 1-1 is the first exercise in the poison prevention project. Exercises 1-2 and 1-3 offer you an opportunity to start working on a project of your own, using the ADDIE model as a framework for ISD.

Section 2 Working Through the ADDIE Model

2 Analysis

Chapter Objectives

At the conclusion of this chapter, you should be able to

- determine the difference between training and nontraining problems
- list three data-gathering steps
- describe two basic components of a focus group and two ground rules for a focus group
- identify the four levels of detail in task analysis
- describe three critical elements of a population analysis
- list at least three instructional methods and their uses.

A Collective Approach

The notion of starting with nothing and finishing with something of value has a great deal of appeal to most of us. Turning a pile of lumber into a house or 10 yards of fabric into curtains demonstrates creativity and manifests a sense of accomplishment. But these efforts don't start in a vacuum. You cannot build a house or sew curtains unless you start with the right raw materials and have enough correct information to successfully complete the project.

Isaac Newton has been quoted as saying that his incredible accomplishments in physics were just the result of his "...standing on the shoulders of giants...." The wisdom and modesty reflected in that statement aside, what Newton was alluding to was the cumulative effect of individual efforts gathered together. Instructional designers do well to identify with the simple truth of this concept: Work with all the best people, gather all the right data, determine how they best fit together, and then design something more significant than each of the single elements alone.

Accumulation of Advantages

Chess masters and other players know that there isn't a single move that can win the game without another move before it that clears the way. World-class players actually think many moves ahead in order to place the pieces exactly where they need them to capture the game. This concept is called an accumulation of advantages. This is exactly the concept that excellent designers use to design a project. One careful move follows another until the project is completed. Designers must think several moves ahead to clear the way for the ADDIE elements to follow. If they skip just one move, they have placed their project in jeopardy.

Instructional designers would be well advised to adapt the legendary curiosity of the cat and a Sherlock Holmesian eagerness to uncover even the most elusive bits of information. This sense of discovery is at the heart of every good designer.

Analysis Basics

The most obvious, and ironically the most neglected, aspect of ISD typically is analysis. For a portfolio full of reasons that sometimes border on embarrassing, analysis has to fight for the respect it deserves in instructional design. Although analysis is often deemed unnecessary, too expensive, or too time consuming, to avoid or neglect the basics of analysis is to design at your own peril. Even the most seemingly obvious analysis questions relating to populations, goals, and resources never find voice and therefore become static and usually questionable constants in an instructional system.

In the analysis stage, instructional designers can never know too much. Curiosity is the first analysis skill that belongs in a designer's tool kit, where it will pay countless dividends. It is impossible to ask too many questions and it is difficult to imagine starting a design project without the essential analysis completed.

Seven key questions require answers during analysis. By addressing each of these questions, instructional designers ensure that they gather all the data they are likely to need as they work their way through the ADDIE system. The questions also help designers check that they have focused on all the possible aspects of the course under consideration. In short, these questions serve as a reality check:

1. What is the need?
2. What is the root cause?

3. What are the goals of the training?
4. What information is needed, and how is it gathered?
5. How will the training be structured and organized?
6. How will the training be delivered?
7. When should training be revised?

The rest of the chapter homes in on each of these questions and highlights some common problems that instructional designers face.

What Is the Need?

Need is the gatekeeper for entry into analysis. If there is no need for the course, there is no need to perform an analysis. This relationship between need and analysis holds true even if a designer has been given an assignment to design a course and has no option except completing it with only two weeks' notice.

Many designers believe that training is the best solution to numerous problems in an organization. Experience shows, however, that some problems do not require training solutions. In fact, they are not training problems at all. For example, the staff at a company may not be communicating with one another. Although they send messages by intranet, the messages are lost in cyberspace and do not reach the intended people. Training will not help those employees improve their communications because the problem is that they need an upgraded intranet system.

A range of issues exists that cannot be fixed with training. Other examples include low wages, miserable working conditions, and the lack of proper equipment. Undoubtedly, there are solutions for these issues, and performance improvement specialists can find ways to solve them. An instructional designer's role in an unhappy work situation should not include designing a course titled "Being Happy With Your Terrible Salary and Lack of Any Tangible Benefits."

Designers must determine early on if training can remedy anything about an apparent problem. If they determine that a training solution is possible, they can move on to the next level of analysis. If they determine that training is not the solution, then they must recognize the reality and move to find other solutions.

The cardinal rule of the analysis element of ISD is this: Make sure there is a training solution before providing one.

Not every need requires training. In the larger world of performance improvement, nontraining solutions are viable and can have a sizable impact. However, within instructional design, the gatekeeper function is critical regardless of the eventual solution. That function enables the designer to get the information needed to make an informed decision.

Typically, designers find that the type of training selected as a solution is based on a learner's lack of knowledge, skills, or abilities, or a combination of these elements.

Training solutions are nearly always available for any performance need that falls within this group. Training does not offer solutions for wages, benefits, working conditions, organizational procedures, or personality conflicts.

What Is the Root Cause?

The first task for a designer is to identify the need and determine the root cause of any problems that exist. Sometimes the need and root cause are relatively easy to uncover. At other times, they may take some digging to reveal. Designers must listen carefully to what they hear and use their logic filter to test each potential issue.

It is important to point out that even though a need appears to be instructional in nature, it might not be. That assessment might be made on the basis of symptoms and not the root cause of the problem. Just as in medicine, treating the symptoms may initially reduce the pain, but it seldom cures the illness.

Following are two situations in which training is not the solution:

- An office is displaying symptoms of discord that are interfering with normal work activities. After some analysis, it is determined that a new supervisor is not working out well with the group. Rather than dealing with the supervisor, management suggests that the training department offer some courses on attitude readjustment and team building. This solution will not solve the problem because it does not touch the root cause—the supervisor.
- At another organization, an undercurrent of sexual harassment problems gained the attention of the executive director. Management expected violations within the organization to diminish or even disappear because of training, but following the training, reports of violations soared. Management blamed the training for the increase. The unexpected result of the training was the empowerment of workers who had experienced problems and now felt obligated to come forward with complaints. The root problem, though, was several individuals who did not see themselves as doing anything offensive.

Here are two situations in which training may be solutions:

- The partners at a law firm are upset about the sudden decline in the quality and quantity of their support staff's work. A senior partner investigates and learns that the office manager has switched word-processing programs. The new software is designed specifically for law offices and requires the staff to learn new computer commands. The office manager chose not to accept the initial training, which the supplier offered at a reduced rate at the time of purchase. The solution now is simple: to give software training to the staff. Unfortunately, the cost for training will be higher than if it had been ordered earlier. The firm is also paying a high cost in the diminished morale.

■ A small, nonprofit group has a yearly fund-raising drive to support its community-based programs. This year the group decided to move from door-to-door solicitation to phone solicitation. Donations are off by more than 30 percent, and the board of directors is livid! The executive director has followed the advice of a consulting firm that has assisted a number of for-profit organizations to improve their sales. Unfortunately, the non-profit group tried to save money by using older volunteers who had trouble reading the calling scripts that were printed in small type. Several approaches could solve this difficulty. A role-playing training class for the volunteers might help them perfect their calls. Another solution might be to enlarge the type on the volunteers' calling sheets.

What Are the Goals of the Training?

Anyone who is going to design a training project must know the rationale for the project. The *rationale* is a mission statement that clearly states the project's reason for existing. It is the heart and soul of the work to be done. The place to start is with the sponsoring department, manager, organization, or client, who can communicate the goals to the designer. Designers need to verify or correct assumptions that may exist. It is important to ask questions such as the following:

■ What does success for this project mean to you?
■ When will you be happy with this project?

The aim is to get to the bottom of the motivational issues because things that may seem trivial to the designer may be a major issue in a project. With projects for internal clients, designers should be sure the results match the unit's goals as well as the goals of the larger organization. By attending to both groups, designers will protect themselves from getting caught in the crossfire if the project does not resonate with the larger organizational goals.

Sometimes the goals of the sponsor and the reality of the content do not make sense, and the designer must step back and find out why. For example, it is not uncommon for an organization to want to use a new technology for training in an effort to look current with the trends in a certain industry although analysis may show that the learners do not need or want a technology-based solution. In this case, the goals of the organization and the reality of the situation do not match. On those occasions, someone may be operating under a hidden and self-interested agenda.

Instructional designers must be alert to the possibility that they may discover problems like these in the populations they serve:

- Career boosting is usually framed by someone whose real interest is in showcasing his or her contribution to management. Evidence that career boosting is at work on a project is often in design that is heavy on production values and low on instructional design values. Training designed for show can often backfire when the cost to produce unnecessary or ineffective training is discovered.
- Getting-even training is discovered when the training goals seem to be, "We'll show them how to..." or "They won't do that to us again!"
- Propaganda training is always designed to send a message to someone. Evidence is that the message is more important than the behavioral objective.

Sound goals designers are likely to see might include an increase of sales by a certain percentage or reduction in the number of mistakes being generated by the implementation of a new software package in an organization.

What Information Is Needed, and How Is It Gathered?

The first three questions helped instructional designers determine that training can address the need and is consistent with individual and organizational goals. Now it is necessary to obtain both *subject matter* and *nonsubject matter.*

Subject matter is the heart of the project, but nonsubject matter is its soul. The information on both will form the basis for the design plan. This book will look at design plans in much more detail in the next chapter.

The nonsubject matter information needed for the design plan includes the rationale for the course, usually described as the goals for the training, population data, course structure, and deliverables. The subject matter information eventually ends up as objectives, evaluation strategies, facilitator prerequisites, and learner prerequisites.

Building a Population Profile. One of the basic tenets of politics is always know the players. A politician would never consider making a move without checking to see how a population of voters felt about a particular issue. A politician would know the *demographic data* that describes the *population,* including age, income, party affiliation, gender, ethnicity, and any other variable that could have an effect on his or her success in the next election. Trainers need to know the players just as much as a politician does. In fact, a trainer's chance at success is just as perilous as a politician's.

A population analysis provides trainers with the information they need to ensure that they communicate in a way their audience will understand. A software training program should not include computer jargon, for example, if the audience is not computer literate.

The first step in identifying the population is to develop a list of all possible factors that could have an impact on designers' thinking and ultimately on their success. Recently, for a project in a foreign country, it was important to analyze differences that would not normally be an issue for designers in a Western country. Some of the factors designers had to consider included

- ■ *Education levels:* Was literacy a concern?
- ■ *Religious influence:* It was important that designers consider prayer times and other religious ceremonies that might conflict with training times.
- ■ *Gender interaction:* Traditional gender roles might create challenges in designing group activities including role-play exercises.
- ■ *Attendance and timing issues:* Many countries are more polychronic (time is more fluid shall we say) than the Western monochromic attitude that expects extreme punctuality.
- ■ *Evaluation techniques:* Some populations might be hesitant to offer opinions or criticism of one another or to question a facilitator.
- ■ *Appropriate materials:* Designers must consider participants' views about how materials represent them, especially graphic representations. The manner of dress and types of activities shown in materials must be acceptable to the target population.
- ■ *Religious/cultural schedules:* In many areas of the world, the normal workweek is not Monday to Friday. Variables like this occur within the individual countries and populations represented in a typical cohort of learners. It is also important not to schedule training during religious holidays that are not familiar to Westerners.

Ultimately this list led to a comprehensive training project that reflected the needs of the population and helped ensure a good start to the design plan. It is important that all the elements in a population study have an effect on the design.

The first step in conducting a population analysis is to establish which of the issues may influence the project's success. A simple matrix, such as the one in table 2-1, works fine for this step. For each element that may have an effect, the designer will say whether it could affect the outcome of the project, why, and whether he or she can do anything about it. The row labeled "Age" shows how someone might complete this table for a course on use of the Internet at a home for senior citizens.

The designer should analyze each of these issues with one question in mind: "Can this element affect the outcome of this project?" For each element, the designer would ask if it has the potential to cause success or failure. Motivation and incentive issues alone can sink a really well-designed training project if they have not been taken into account. If the answer is yes, it can cause success or failure, the designer must address why, and then what he or she is going to do about it.

Table 2-1. Population analysis.

Issue	Influences Success? Yes or No	Why?	What Can I Do?
Age	Yes	Seniors may not have experience using computers, let alone the Internet.	Split the class into two groups—those with computer experience and those without.
Culture			
Education Level			
Ethnicity			
Gender			
Incentive			
Language Skill			
Motivation			

Designing and Conducting a Focus Group. Every instructional designer should be familiar with focus groups and the value they bring to analysis and evaluation. Focus groups range from informal conversations to videotaped productions, and there are almost as many styles as there are designers to facilitate them. The term *focus group* derives from the intent of this analysis tool, which is to focus on a particular topic and capture participants' comments.

Focus groups are used widely for gauging participants' views on such diverse topics as a political issue or a new product being brought to market. An instructional designer might be interested in using this tool to determine a population's attitudes about a proposed training strategy or to uncover issues that cause problems in a work group.

Regardless of the content or style of a focus group, its single most important component is the facilitator. Each focus group requires a facilitator who remains comfortable if tensions arise (as they surely do) when participants express strong opinions and who is responsible enough to maintain control. It is painful to see an inexperienced facilitator buckle under the pressure of two or more opinionated participants who take over the process.

The focus-group process presented here represents the author's experience with these groups in a training setting. Designers will undoubtedly evolve their own strategies and even change them as conditions warrant.

In general, focus groups tend to be useful in data-gathering situations that involve emotions, human interactions, and attitudes. They are also a very powerful problem-solving tool.

Every focus group should have at least four basic components: ground rules, warm-up questions, focus questions, and closers. Following are descriptions of each.

■ *Ground rules:* Ground rules set the code of conduct for the group, both in terms of topic and process. Ground rules should be clearly stated and should appear on an easel sheet or in any other visible place. Common ground rules governing process include time limits on the length of the focus group activity and time limits on individual comments. Topic boundaries include facilitator privilege, such as the authority to moderate as necessary, and confidentiality and nonconfidentiality statements. Time limits are an absolute necessity for most focus groups although it is sometimes tricky to gauge the time needed to collect data. Time limits assist in focusing participants' thoughts on the topic and help enforce participant and topic boundaries. Typical phrases to move the discussion along are "I'm sorry we must move on or we will run out of time" or "It sounds like we've hit on a hot topic. We could go on indefinitely, but we have a lot on our plate today; for now we need to move on so that we can meet our session objectives." Individual comments should be limited to 90 seconds or less. Longer comments become speeches, and if one participant is perceived as being in control, others may feel stifled or unimportant. It is sometimes useful to ask participants to think and respond as if they were writing bulleted comments on the topic. If focus groups are to be a success, it is vitally important to set topic boundaries and enforce them. Facilitators must limit the questions to one or a few topics and let participants know they will be cut off if they wander from them. A focus group concerning workload, for example, can quickly turn into a history of the industrial age. It usually only takes one corrective maneuver to keep that from happening. Facilitator privilege is the right to control the focus group process. The facilitator is the traffic cop of the focus group. There can be no compromise on this component or the facilitator may quickly lose control of the group.

Confidentiality must also be addressed. The decision to record, transcribe, or otherwise document the group's actions will have an effect on the outcome. Some participants may want comments on record to substantiate a particular view about the topic, whereas others will not feel comfortable saying anything of value if it will be attributed to them. Designers need to discuss these perspectives with a client to eliminate any misunderstanding before the session is held. No matter which choice designers make, they must inform the participants.

■ *Warm-up questions:* Facilitators usually use warm-up questions to get a group talking and thinking. Some designers call these *framing questions* because they open the gate for participants to enter and frame the rest of the process. Venting is a key element of this early stage of the focus group. Hidden agendas and bottled-up frustrations come to the surface and must be vented or they could damage the focus group. Thirty seconds of griping at this early stage is seldom a problem. Thirty seconds later may negate the entire session. If a focus group is considering members' attitudes about a new process or procedure, a warm-up question might ask them about their feelings toward change in general. For example, for a focus group about workplace change, the warm-up question might be, "How are things going in the office right now?" or "What is the hot topic of discussion right now?" These warm-up questions start to frame the context of the issue. Immediately the participants know the general direction in which the facilitator is heading. If the participants express tension, anxiety, or anger at this point, the facilitator at least has a barometer of the level of emotion that the topic is generating. Eventually the facilitator will get to the subject, usually with the pressure removed to a degree that allows for an excellent focus group.

■ *Focus questions:* This section is the heart of a focus group. All of the activity before and after supports this set of questions. Designers should first work on these questions as they begin designing their focus groups. Then they can build everything around them. In a group focusing on workplace change, for example, the designer would be interested in the participants' reaction to proposed or suggested changes. The designer might offer a range of options for the groups' reaction, or the designer might build toward one predefined series of changes that an organization might be considering and gauge the participants' reaction. Either way, the focus questions are the most important of all the questions. If a company is asking about change because it wants to introduce work in teams, for example, the designer might ask, "How do you feel about working in teams?" or "What do you think of the following types of changes?" These questions are different ways of getting to the main point. Facilitators will explore the focus questions in more depth as they begin to gauge the reactions and comments. They sometimes find it useful to narrow the scope of the discussion until they find the level of "no further usefulness."

■ *Closers:* A successful close requires a smooth transition. A final question allows participants to bring the topic to closure. Facilitators should ask questions that require some thought and let the participants know that they have been listening to what they say. Here are some examples of closers that include elements of ownership, leadership, and empowerment:

— "If you have the opportunity to say one thing to the boss about this topic, what would it be?"

— "If you were the boss and could do one thing about this situation, what would it be?"

— "You have just been put in charge of fixing this situation, what is your first step?"

■ *Other focus group issues:* Some other important issues include attendance by nonparticipants, location, size, and makeup. Many times people are so interested in the process or consider themselves significant enough stakeholders that they demand to be part of the facilitation. This is generally a bad idea, especially if the person sitting in is a stakeholder in the discussion. The presence of a manager or outspoken observer can change the tone of a group. Occasionally, a stakeholder offers input or answers the questions and skews the results of the session entirely. The location of the focus group process is also important. If a topic is controversial and opinions may end up being polarized, facilitators should move to a neutral site. The home field advantage is really a disadvantage in some situations. For example, a labor-management topic is best handled on a neutral site to avoid the appearance of managerial influence of the group. Facilitators should not be afraid to move to a new venue if the conditions warrant and the budget allows for it. Even a move across the street to a hotel or restaurant can make the difference between getting what they need or making the problem worse. A move might make participants in a labor-management focus group more willing to say what they are thinking, whereas they might supply stock answers or not participate at all if they are at a stakeholder's environment. It is important that the focus group resemble the population it is analyzing. Fine-tuning the size and makeup can be a challenge. In some groups this is easy because the focus groups are themselves the entire population. In larger populations, facilitators need to determine which variables are important to the content and assemble their participants in a way that represents those interests. For example, if the population for a focus group on the issue of day care in the workplace is not influenced by age, then age should not be a sampling standard. Gender might very well be a sampling condition. Other qualifiers might be job title, seniority, education, and ethnicity; in fact, anything that might engender a difference of opinion could be a qualifier.

Developing Surveys. Every instructional designer uses surveys; how designers use them can determine success or failure. How questions are asked is the key. Open-ended questions lead to open-ended answers, but for *quantifiable data,* designers must ask quantifiable questions and supply specific ranges of answers. For example, a designer who wants to ask 100 workers about their ability to use a specific software package might ask either of these questions:

- How well can you use the software?
- How well can you use the software? (a) very well, (b) know most of the commands I need, (c) struggle with some commands, (d) not very much, (e) not at all.

In the first example, the designer will get a range of answers that cannot be easily compared with each other or a standard from which to start designing. The designer who asks the second question will be able to compute percentages and use those data to design the course based on quantifiable data. If 50 percent say they know the software very well and 20 percent say not very much, the designer can eliminate the top 50 percent and concentrate on the bottom 50 percent who need skill enhancement.

Rating questions also are useful to providing insight into content. For example, a designer might ask: "How do you rate your ability to perform the following functions using the software: Mail merge (a) flawlessly, (b) few problems, (c) many problems, (d) cannot use it at all." The designer would then ask about all of the commands or skills that might be considered content in the course. The designer will build the basis of the content for the course as he or she works through the questions. This same process works for almost any skill-based analysis.

For sampling *attitudes,* designers can also turn to surveys and change the style of questions to some degree. In the case of a workplace in chaos, the questions might be:

- How would you rate the number of interpersonal problems in the office? (a) no problems, (b) some minor problems, (c) many problems, (d) nothing but problems.
- In your opinion, what is the atmosphere like in the office? (a) no tension, (b) some tension, (c) very tense, (d) chaos.

Using SMEs. The abbreviation SMEs stands for *subject matter experts,* whom designers like to call "shmees." Some instructional designers work with SMEs regularly, whereas others never work with them. The need for SMEs varies with the kind of instructional design.

Working with SMEs is an art in itself. The designer's tool of working effectively with SMEs is a valuable one to enhance or develop.

SMEs fall in one of two types of general category. Some have expertise in a specific skill, such as painting or electrical work, and are brought on to a project to provide data for apprenticeship materials, procedural manuals, or another aspect of the project. Many of these SMEs have never done any type of design work before. Designers must be sure that they are clear as to what information they are asking the SMEs to provide, especially those who are new to the design process. Working with objectives and evaluations might be new to them, and it is important that they realize that they only need to provide technical information and that the designer will take care of the rest.

The other kind of SME is more academic, and the project typically is the result of research or experience gained in the field, or both. They are brought to a project to offer expertise in specialized areas. This group is likely to include professionals with advanced degrees and academic standing. Clear lines of demarcation and responsibility are vital. It is also important that the designers in this environment have both the decision-making authority and responsibility for instructional design issues.

One of the most important keys to working with SMEs is clarity. Most are eager to work on instructional design projects and just need to know the rules. Everyone likes to have his or her knowledge and experience recognized and used. Working with designers should be a great experience for them, and once they realize that the designers are there to provide the instructional framework, they can relax and concentrate on the content.

It is critically important to choose the right SMEs. The following rules are a useful guide to making the selection:

1. Only use SMEs with recent (within the past year) experience in the content area. At the current pace of change in most fields, people who have not been working in the field during the past year are probably not sufficiently up to date on knowledge and practice. Every field of study is different, but most change considerably in a year.
2. Ask around and find out which SMEs are considered the best by others in the peer group.
3. Interview before deciding to help eliminate possible personality conflicts.

4. Determine if the SMEs have the time to devote to the design process.
5. Determine how SMEs will be compensated before starting.
6. Review and resolve any copyright issues with SMEs before starting.
7. If relevant, ask for writing samples or previous content-related materials.
8. Determine if any previous instructional design experience exists.

A little time in finding the best SMEs early in the process may eliminate an irrevocable error later during your project.

There are three basic models for the roles of designers in curriculum development:

■ The designer is the only person involved and is the SME.
■ The designer has some subject matter knowledge but works with SMEs.
■ The designer has little, if any, subject matter knowledge and relies on SMEs for assistance.

The power of excellent training comes not from subject matter content, but from the ISD process that designs, implements, and evaluates that training. Anyone who doubts the truth of that statement should compare training programs in any field that are designed using ISD and those that are not. The contrast is obvious.

How Will the Training Be Structured and Organized?

Task analysis is the grandparent of all analysis methods. It involves the process of breaking down a job or assignment into each task associated with it to learn the skills and knowledge necessary to perform it. The data gathered in this process assist the designer in building the structure of the project, including instructional methods and media. They also tell how best to organize objectives and evaluations in a logical continuum from beginning to end.

Task analysis is something every instructional designer does and can be used for a variety of situations. Jobs, skills, procedures, processes, and, of course, tasks are usually best analyzed in this manner. Task analysis is the first step for an instructional designer who needs to replicate anything that involves human interaction in a series of steps. An instructional designer would perform a task analysis to be sure a lesson covers every step a person needs to know to perform the job, skill, procedure, process, or task.

Conducting a Task Analysis. Even though it is such a fundamental tool of the instructional designer, task analysis is often done poorly or given little preparation time. In fact, it is not as simple as one might assume. Four levels of detail exist in a task analysis: job, task, skill, and subskill as shown in the accompanying "Task Analysis Examples."

> **Task Analysis Examples**
>
> Following are examples of task analysis for an air traffic controller and a sales executive.
>
> - **Job:** air traffic controller
>   — **Task:** giving an airplane clearance to land at an airport
>   — **Skills:** monitoring a number of data screens and looking out the window of the tower
>   — **Subskill:** checking the radar screen for possible problems.
> - **Job:** vice president of sales
>   — **Task:** monthly reporting
>   — **Skills:** gathering data, writing the report, and so forth
>   — **Subskill:** accessing the organization's spreadsheets and locating the sales figures.

Some instructional designers spend most of their professional life working in situations that require them to follow technical task-analysis procedures. Imagine trying to perform a task analysis on a job like that of manager of an energy-producing nuclear reactor. That job involves numerous tasks that must be replicated exactly the way they are engineered because a misstep in the task analysis could put people's lives in jeopardy. Consider what would happen if a task analysis missed a key step in a safety procedure. As a result of that omission, employees might not receive training for a specific problem that might occur. No training probably means diminished effectiveness in dealing with the problem.

Several steps are vitally important in task analysis from the perspective of a designer:

1. *Define the target of the analysis:* With whom are you going to work? What titles or responsibilities do you want to analyze?
2. *Choose the methodology:* Will you use task analysis, focus groups, or other methods of analysis?
3. *Select the analysis subjects:* Choose the best candidates for analysis. Typically, these are the people who actually do the work and are considered the best at it. It helps to work with several individuals who are struggling with a task so designers can see why they are having trouble.

Task Analysis Field Visit. One of the best ways to learn the art of task analysis is to go into the real world and give it a try. This isn't nearly as difficult as it may seem at first. Designers actually perform task analysis many times a day without thinking about it. A good example might be standing in line to use an unfamiliar automated teller machine. As people work their way up the line, they are actually doing task analysis as they watch those in front operate the machine. Each time one person performs an operation, people in line are observing and remembering how it is done. People in line—those analyzing—note when someone makes a mistake and remember to avoid those same errors.

How Will the Training Be Delivered?

Instructional designers need to determine the instructional methods and distribution methods they will be working with early in their planning, sometimes before really starting the project. Instructional designers make choices that determine how their learners interact with the subject matter. The designer's tool of matching innovative distribution methods and instructional methods is important. It is essential that these two elements be in place before designers get too involved with the design phase.

Possible Instructional Methods. *Instructional methods* are techniques that designers use to link objectives with learners. Lectures, group discussions, and case studies all serve as the link between the learner and subject matter, much the same way as a book or webpage links information with the end user.

These are some of the more frequently used instructional methods:

- *Lecture:* With few exceptions, instructional designers should only use lectures in combination with other methods. They might use them alone if they have an inspirational facilitator and want to inspire learners. Otherwise, learners will be fighting back yawns and hunger pains while a facilitator is lecturing. With lectures, it is important to have in place the design elements of clear time limits as well as liberal use of visuals or other stimulators.
- *Role play:* In role plays, learners enact the roles of people placed in various situations in an effort to closely match the training with the real world. Role plays are a great way of placing learners in the action of solving a problem or practicing a skill. Instructional designers must be mindful of any issues that could cause problems if they use role playing with a group of introverts or a population facing some physical or emotional challenges. Designers must take the time to prepare both the role and scenario descriptions and very precise instructions to both learners and facilitators.
- *Case study:* This method moves the learner up the cognitive ladder and requires decisions, either in a group or singularly. Case studies are great ways to provide instruction in cognitive skills like negotiating, facilitating, reasoning, and constructing solutions. Instructional designers must be careful to ensure that the cases are relevant to their learners. If the cases

are out of the learners' contextual framework, they are not likely to hold the learners' interest. It is vitally important that the instructor provides complete case studies, not just bits and pieces of a case. Incomplete information can easily turn a case intended to illustrate a marketing challenge into a case solved by the company giving employees two weeks additional vacation every year. For example, a case study might say that employees were working without any days off, but it might fail to mention that the extra work was because the office was being moved to another building. Without providing complete information, readers may be sympathetic to the workers and want to give them extra vacation.

▪ *Simulations:* Practice, practice, and more practice. Simulation is one of the best methods for getting learners to practice a skill, process, task, or procedure. It is also great for psychomotor skills. Simulations are the process of performing a task in a safe environment. They are especially helpful for dangerous or expensive tasks. Psychomotor objectives are exercised in simulations because there is no chance of damaging expensive equipment or injuring a participant in a dangerous procedure.

▪ *Gaming:* Gaming is the process of placing participants in the position of having multiple choices to make in an exercise that borders on real life but provides the safety of a simulation. Just as video games simulate some level of reality, gaming provides the same safe environment without subjecting participants to the dangers of actually performing a task. Some of the best gaming is sophisticated and reaches the limits of technology. Many military applications are right at the corner of reality and surrealism.

▪ *Critical incident:* This method is used in many training areas that challenge the ability of a learner to react quickly to a problem. Essentially, this is a version of a case study, but it leaves out some of the key data. Airline pilots are subjected to critical incident methods when they simulate flights that develop problems. The extensive use of flight data recorders has allowed the advancement of this method in transportation training.

▪ *Drill:* Keep doing it, doing it, doing it. Drills are used extensively in computer-based training. For example, many programs require learners to enter words or numbers numerous times to complete a sentence or math problem.

▪ *Job aid:* This training method pays great dividends in many projects. Job aids are any materials that workers keep at hand for easy reference, such as a printed form, cheat sheet, or procedures manual, that contains information on a concept or skill. Since our memory is often unreliable, it is useful to have something in hand that supports the concept or skill involved. Job aids can many times stand on their own and not require any class or technology time to implement.

■ *Critique:* This is a modified case study approach that requires determining the strengths and weaknesses of a situation or process, then finding a solution. An annual review by a boss is a valid instructional method.

■ *Discussion:* In this context, discussion is directed, follows another activity, and creates the environment for interactivity. The discussions may be large group, small group, buzz groups, or teams. Generally, the discussion should not involve groups larger than 25 or 30 learners. If size is an issue, the group should be broken down into workable chunks. It is important that instructional designers prepare both the facilitator and learners before any discussion starts so they know what they will be discussing and why. Without direction or preparation, the group may wander off the subject.

■ *In-basket:* Learners participate by working through a pile of data sitting in front of them, usually on a desk. They have to make decisions about each item, and the results offer a snapshot of their ability to solve problems. This method usually incorporates a degree of role-play and case-study methods.

■ *On-the-job training:* On-the-job training (OJT) is probably the most often used instructional method. Some organizations realize they are using it, but others—those that have an employee probation period—may not realize that they're using it. OJT is intended to be mentoring in its purest form. Instructional designers must ensure that this method does not preclude use of others.

■ *Brainstorming:* This method asks learners to build experience into creativity by developing ideas on a specific subject with other colleagues. It can be tough to pull off and sometimes even tougher to design because it is free-wheeling. Brainstorming sessions should never last more than 10 minutes, and facilitators should be given enough ideas for refocusing if the group becomes lethargic. Designers need to accept the fact that brainstorming may backfire on the facilitator and that these sessions have the potential to have a negative impact on the success of the project if the process bogs down in political or emotional responses. For example, a group that is working to find new ideas for a marketing campaign may end up blaming engineering for never having the right product available when the market peaks. It becomes important, therefore, that a facilitator be prepared to nudge the group back on track and away from a negative ending.

Other methods that are related directly to technology are computer-based training (CBT), multimedia, interactive TV, teleconferencing, groupware, virtual reality, and employee performance support systems (EPSSs).

Instructional Methods to Avoid. There are three instructional methods to avoid:

- *Undirected groups:* This method is usually little more than groups discussing a topic or subject matter with little or no direction by a facilitator. It is typically used to kill time and offers little, if any, instructional value.
- *Unguided missile:* This seldom-used method usually begins with this statement from the facilitator at a training session: "Now, let's decide what we are going to do today." Although it may appear that there is a positive in getting group consensus for objectives, the method is an abandonment of instructional principles.
- *Theory tantrums:* Instructors must not dwell on theory. Training courses can only stand the smallest bits of theory when they substantiate a point or set the groundwork for something that follows. Always turn theory into practice.

Types of Distribution Methods. *Distribution methods* are the ways designers deliver the instructional methods. Proper matching of distribution and instructional methods and platforms also saves time and energy, both for the designer and the learner. A number of distribution methods are widely used for training. The ones presented here are just a starting point for the discussion:

- *Captive audience:* Otherwise known as *classroom training,* this is the most common way to administer training. It consists of one or more learners with one or more facilitators in a single location using no technologies.
- *Technology-enhanced:* This is the name for training that makes use of an overhead, slide projector, or laptop and computer projector. One or more technologies assist in the implementation of the course.
- *Technology-facilitated:* This is what is commonly referred to by several hundred different terms such as multimedia, CBT, e-learning, or virtual reality. This platform is delivered with the technology, learner, and perhaps a facilitator in one location with the technology serving the dominant role in facilitation.
- *Distance learning:* This term describes the method in which learners are at one or more different physical locations than the source of the instruction. Teleconferencing is an example of distance learning.
- *Distributed learning:* Home study courses are an example of this method. Training is distributed using a process, such as mail, that is not related to the implementation.

Other distribution methods include cable television, CD-ROM, email, extranets, Internet, intranets, local area networks (LANs), satellite television, simulators, voicemail, wide area networks (WANs), and the World Wide Web.

Learning technologies may be *synchronous* or *asynchronous*. Synchronous learning assumes that the learning and the facilitation take place at the same time. A good example is a chat room on the Internet. Everyone is participating in real time, and learners are usually expected to participate at a set time, much as a regular training course. Asynchronous training allows late sleepers and night owls to participate in training. Learners have a choice of when they participate as one benefit of the technology. Learning is sometimes implemented as an email system or a forum on a computer server.

When Should Training Be Revised?

Since the inception of the atomic age, most of us have become familiar with the term *half-life.* It refers to how long half of the atoms in a radioactive substance will continue to emit radiation before they disintegrate. It has also taken on a more cultural meaning. For instructional designers, the term refers to the fact that data gathered in analysis has a half-life, or period of validity. In some topic areas, the useful life of the data is measured in centuries. In others, it can literally be measured in seconds or minutes. In instructional design, half-life means the time it takes for a noticeable or significant change in data to take place.

It is important to note that this does not apply to all of the data becoming useless, but only enough of it to render the training suspect or dated. It may only take one incorrect element of the subject matter to ruin weeks of work by a designer. This obsolescence is particularly noticeable in computer and web-based instruction. It is not uncommon for the design project to outlast the technology. A designer may, for example, design a computer-based training project on the basis of a certain hardware and software platform that could easily be at least a generation old when it is implemented.

To prevent this technology advancement from affecting a design, designers should ask the following data-decay rating questions for each element of the project that may be affected. Respond with a rating from 0 to 5 (lowest to highest):

- How critical is the data to the success of the training?
- How likely is it that the data will change?
- How easy is it to update data internally?
- Can learners or trainers easily obtain updated data?

If the analysis of the decay rating elements ends up being near the low end of the scale, designers should consider a process that allows for updating. This can be as easy as providing a webpage for updated information or distributing data sheets as necessary. In either case, designers should not assume that a completed project will rest comfortably on the information provided, unless they have determined that to be case.

Common Problems and Solutions

Knowing some of problems that are frequently encountered in ISD can help designers avoid them—or fix them early in the process.

Too Much or Too Little Content

Instructional designers rarely have the luxury of exactly matching the amount of content with the time available for implementation. It is common for designers to have three days of content for a two-hour implementation requirement or 20 minutes of content for an eight-hour window. An effective way to solve the information overload problem is for the designer to call a meeting of all stakeholders in the training and marshal all the facts and data possible about the training.

At the meeting, the designer should take the following steps toward a consensus decision on the content:

1. Cluster the data into topic areas.
2. Rank-order the topic areas.
3. Assign priorities to the data within each topic area.
4. Decide which topics and subtopics cannot be eliminated.
5. Review all topics and subtopics for redundancy.
6. Combine and eliminate subtopics as necessary.
7. Estimate timing on the topic areas and on each subtopic.
8. Map out a project plan and outline each topic with the subtopics underneath them.
9. Delineate the topics and subtopics with time indications so that it is obvious which ones will remain using different options.

If too little content remains, designers should review what they have to make sure they aren't missing something. If nothing is missing, they should try breaking the topics down into smaller chunks to see if it is possible to include more. It may also be possible to shorten the implementation time. It is never a good idea to waste a learner's time. Everyone can tell when instructors are stretching content. Designers need to offer realistic expectations for keeping this problem from surfacing.

When Training Is Mandated

Mandated training is an exception to the rules for both too much and too little information. Designers often have little leeway in designing around obvious mismatches. Designers should think about these things before they move to the design stage:

- Have you really determined the problem, gap, or need?
- Have you determined if it is training or nontraining?
- Have you gathered data?
- Have you considered using one or all of these analysis methods to gather data?
  — focus group
  — surveys
  — task analysis
  — SME group
- Who are your SMEs?
- What are the constraints and resources?
- Have you determined all of the organizational needs?
- Have you reviewed your distribution and instructional methods?
- Do you know the half-life of your content?
- Do you have too much or too little content?

In Conclusion

In this chapter, you have learned about the analysis stage of instructional systems design. During analysis, designers must determine the answers to seven crucial questions. They must determine the need for instructional design and decide whether training is the right solution for responding to that need. Their analyses require them to explore the goals of the training and to gather information from population analyses, focus groups, surveys, and other sources. During this stage, they will conduct task analyses, which will help them to formulate the structure of their projects, and they will consider which instructional methods make sense. Before they begin designing their project, designers must also consider whether it is likely to be dated. Analysis requires a broad look ahead.

If you have any trouble, go back to the appropriate section in the book for review.

Putting What You Have Learned Into Action

Now, let's work through some analysis exercises—exercises 2-1 to 2-11 on the CD—to build your confidence and start you on the road to designing a project of your own. The exercises cover these topics:

- ✓ determining the need
- ✓ carrying out population analysis
- ✓ conducting surveys
- ✓ conducting a task analysis
- ✓ choosing the right instructional method
- ✓ knowing when to revise a project
- ✓ getting ready for design.

3 Design: Mastering Objectives

Chapter Objectives

At the conclusion of this chapter, you should be able to

- name the four classifications of objectives
- differentiate among draft, process, terminal, and enabling objectives
- write at least one example of draft, process, terminal, and enabling objectives
- describe the four different objective domains
- define the performance agreement principle

Why Objectives?

Objectives are the conceptual and operational framework that inspires and sustains the instructional design process. Without them, education and training have little more than content and contemplation to assure quality. From the perspective of an instructional designer, the art of writing objectives is a fundamental and irreplaceable skill that requires nurture, reflection, and practice for competence.

Objectives are the nucleus of every aspect of instructional design. Designers who can write superb objectives seldom have trouble with other elements of the process. By the same token, if a designer's project seems unbalanced or some aspects of it are not working, he or she should first look at the objectives. Almost all design problems start with sloppy or nonexistent objectives. Valuing the components embodied in objectives forces a designer to transform vague goals into observable behaviors. If you learn only one skill as an instructional designer, make it writing great objectives.

Traditional approaches to writing objectives focus primarily on the behavioral aspects of the topic and you will find incredibly detailed coverage of both terminal and enabling objectives in this chapter. In addition, you will also be exposed to two new classifications of objectives that assist instructional designers with the design process itself. *Draft* and *process objectives* expand the role of objectives in instructional design and offer designers two more tools to build their skills.

Four Classifications of Objectives

To make the process of instructional design more efficient, it may help you to think of objectives as existing in four classifications. Two are informal and used primarily during the design process; these are aptly named draft objectives and process objectives. The two more traditional classifications of *terminal objectives* and *enabling objectives* usually find a home in the formal design process in your design and lesson plans.

Before you reach the point of formalizing objectives into three or four element terminal and enabling categories, you are often working in a less formal design setting. In this environment it helps to have less formal ways of expressing behaviors than when the objectives have matured and are ready to be written in the *A-B-C-D format,* meaning audience, behaviors, condition, and degree.

The challenges that exist in using a formal objective structure early in the design process are often related to two diverse issues; the first is trying to capture and reflect goals more directly in objectives and the second is the ability of a designer to work more efficiently with nondesign populations, including SMEs, clients, and others involved in the design and development process. This is where the use of draft and process objectives makes good sense.

Draft Objectives

Draft objectives are the younger sibling of the formal terminal and enabling behavioral objective statements of what a learner should be able to accomplish at the end of a course, module, or program. Draft objectives are meant to be the bridge between initially identifying concepts and skills within a design and later writing formal objectives. They are an excellent way of working with SMEs and others using nontechnical terms or processes and yet allow a designer to gather the data necessary to drill down to the more technical detail necessary for a design plan.

In comparison to formal objectives, there are two main differences in the way these are written. Draft objectives are not expected to contain audience, condition, or degree statements, or even well-defined behaviors. Additionally, draft objectives are not necessarily grouped or subdivided into terminal and enabling categories.

Draft objectives are written to reflect individual learning episodes, and they may or may not be initially grouped with other objectives to build more traditional terminal and enabling status. The process of grouping and categorizing comes after the process of writing draft objectives. Examples of draft objectives for a course in the content area of instructional design might be

- Define the term "system."
- List the elements of the ADDIE ISD model.
- Give an example of designer activities in each element of the ADDIE model.
- List the four parts of an objective.
- Define the term "terminal objective."
- Define the term "enabling objective."
- Write terminal objectives.
- Write enabling objectives.
- List the elements in a design plan.
- Prepare a draft rationale for a course or program.

An example of grouped draft objectives for the same ISD course in the content area of prerequisites would be

- Define the term "prerequisite."
- Define the term "facilitator prerequisite."
- List examples of facilitator prerequisites.
- Define the term "participant prerequisite."
- List examples of participant prerequisites.

Process Objectives

Process objectives are general expressions of direction or outcome that do not necessarily reflect specific learner performance or behavior, yet are important considerations for the designer to keep in mind during the design process. Although some process objectives may seem like traditional goals, a process objective provides clear direction to the design process. Goals are general statements whereas process objectives are more concrete, yet they do not contain the level of detail that behavioral objectives do. Once again, process objectives allow for a more efficient connection with nondesigners participating in the design process. Examples of process objectives for a project might be

- Building learner identity with the sponsor is important.
- Case study examples must be written using content derived from actual cases.
- Excellent facilitation skills required for this content.
- Learner motivation issues must be addressed early in this course.

Process objectives are not only one of the building blocks of instructional design but are the foundation for building a solid working relationship with clients and other professionals in the design process. In some ways they are the Rosetta stone of this process; they allow an avenue for translation for the many participants in the process. Everyone's ideas and suggestions have a common language, and the language and operating environment of each participant are translated readily into tangible discussion and action points.

Imagine having a design team that consists of one instructional designer, one client representative, one writer, and one media designer. Depending on the experience of each of these individuals with the design process, you might encounter a range of communications and project "style" challenges. By starting with a common set of process objectives, a designer will be able to start the project with an informal set of guidelines. Because this preliminary step involves reducing these ideas to writing, you not only have a paper trail but also have tangible points for discussion if everyone isn't on the same page in the design or project process. This element of the process alone can save a project, as well as many hours or days of frustration and misunderstanding among participants.

Terminal and Enabling Objectives

Behavioral objectives are the bread and butter of the instructional design profession. A course without objectives is a course without direction and usually lacks any depth or credibility. In ISD, formal behavioral objectives are classified as either terminal or enabling, depending on an individual objective's placement in a design plan. *Terminal objectives* are just that; they define terminal or exit competencies expected of a learner at the end of a course, module, or program. *Enabling objectives* are the supporting behaviors that, when grouped together, build the path to the terminal objectives.

Behavioral objectives should always be written in the A-B-C-D format. The one exception to this rule is for enabling objectives, which don't always require an audience statement. In all cases, terminal and enabling objectives must provide a formal, well-written framework that allows design projects to grow and mature.

Behavioral Objective Basics

Designers frame objectives from the perspective of the end user of the training, not the facilitator. They do not say what a facilitator is supposed to do, but what the learner should be able to do at the end of the course. It would not be correct to say, "The facilitator will teach the students how to use the fax machine" or "At the end of this course, the facilitator will have presented all of the course materials in a friendly and persuasive manner." Learners are the focus of objectives because they are the reason for the course. Although directions to a facilitator are important to instructional design, they say nothing about what the leaner is supposed to do at the end of the course.

Objectives are written at the level of an individual learner. Writing an objective that describes more than one learner presents a number of design issues, the least of which is how designers provide any meaningful evaluation. It is also problematic for a designer to think of an entire subset of learners as if they were a single learner. To do so challenges clarity. An objective for a group project can be written at the level of the single learner.

Following is an objective for a group:

■ Given paint, brushes, and a bare wall, the apprentices in the Painting for Pleasure course will create a mural with the dimensions of at least 4 feet by 4 feet.

Better is this group objective:

■ Given paint, brushes, and a bare wall, an apprentice in the Painting for Pleasure course will create a mural element with other apprentices each of whom contributes at least one section of the completed work.

The second objective makes it possible for each learner to be evaluated on his or her individual accomplishment, without relying on other learners. Following is a learner-centered version of an objective on use of a fax machine:

■ Given a working fax machine, the Office Technology participant should be able to send a two-page fax to another location without error.

Objectives are necessary for each learning activity. Every concept, skill, or objective-worthy behavior needs to be identified and honored with an objective. If an activity is important enough to be included in a design plan, then it is important enough to have a written objective. An objective is the best way to guarantee that the designer will be able to evaluate whether course participants have mastered each skill or concept for which there is instruction. Designers have a tendency to write either too many or too few objectives. They can decide if they need to write an objective by answering the question, "Does it stand on its own?"

Objectives Are Not Goals

Goals and objectives are not the same things. *Goals* are general statements of desired outcomes, whereas *objectives* are detailed statements of outcomes. Draft and process objectives are a much closer fit for expressing these interests. For example, a process objective might be to improve communications within an organization, whereas an enabling or terminal objective for that design need might be

■ Given several role-play situations and class discussions, the Better Communications participant should be able to develop at least three specific ways to improve intraoffice communications.

Designers should write objectives so that they can be met within the implementation time of the course. This is a nice way of saying, "Don't promise something you have no control over." Setting an objective that states that a learner "...should be able to construct an effective marketing plan" is much different from an objective that promises "increased sales in six months." Designers only have control over the process of training a learner to assemble a marketing plan; they cannot influence sales volume.

What Objectives Should Be

Objectives should be *measurable* and *observable*. An objective that cannot be measured or observed is probably not going to have much chance for evaluation. That shortcoming significantly diminishes the usefulness of the objective.

Several different methods are available for writing objectives. The most recognized format contains the elements of the previously mentioned A-B-C-D format (audience, behavior, condition, and degree). Some other formats require a fifth element, whereas still others require only three. The adding and subtracting of elements is usually the result of adding more detail to a behavior or eliminating the audience element.

The Four Elements of an Objective

Theorists and practitioners have used a variety of formats for objectives. ISD allows designers to adjust their process to meet their needs, and not all of them use the A-B-C-D format. Nevertheless, designers should never undertake the process of designing objectives without reviewing the four elements as part of the procedure. If they consider audience, behavior, condition, and degree as they design their objectives, they are halfway to a successful design. Following are descriptions of each of the elements.

Audience

What must appear as the most obvious of the objective elements—the audience—is crucial to writing objectives. Designers must validate the audience for each objective. Just as the term "student" may refer to someone in kindergarten or high school, so may the terms "learner" and "participant" refer to different groups. Designers must make sure that the audience statement is specific to the course and intended population.

The deceivingly simple concept of audience in instructional design is much more complex than just naming a population. What really is important is making sure that you have accurately and concisely described your audience. The crucial element of the audience objective element is the knowledge a designer gathers from such diverse sources as population profiles and SMEs. Just as with many other aspects of instructional design, the audience statement is the product of a designer's analysis of the target population. The designer must validate the audience for each objective with data gathered from many other sources.

The description of the audience should be specific by using the course title or another characteristic, such as:

- The New Methods in Marketing participant
- learner in Handling Stress on the Job
- Local 786 apprentice painter
- Software for Cynics student.

Behavior

Without any meaningful statement of behavior, both formal objectives and training itself are pointless. *Behavior* is the culmination of all the analysis and the purpose for evaluation. A close examination of a behavior statement in an objective reveals a vivid description of an anticipated outcome. When trainers predict that a learner should be able to do something, the designer is drawing the finish line for every learner.

Most behavior statements are worded in the format "should be able to _____" or "will be able to _____." Designers must be careful about which of these formats they choose for writing their objectives. "Will" and "should" have two distinctly different meanings, and the selection is more than just stylistic. Promising that a learner will be able to do something is much different than stating one should be able to do something. The argument against "will" is based on the concept of promising absolute results. For example, if an objective states that the "The Golfing for Beginners participant will be able to score in the low 60s for 18 holes of golf," the designer had better have one great golf program developed! *Designers should not make promises they cannot keep.*

The behavior statement must not use verbs such as "learn" and "understand" because there is no way to measure or observe them. Just because a learner's frequent nods and thoughtful looks give the facilitator reason to believe that he or she is learning and understanding does not make it true. Behavior needs to be observable and measurable. Verbs such as "create," "write," "list," "construct," and "repair" are observable, measurable, and suitable for statements of behavior in written objectives. Table 3-1 offers more examples of verbs that work well in behavior statements.

Statements involving psychomotor behavior include "pull," "hold," "turn," "tighten," and "rotate." Don't worry about not seeing these verbs and others like them in the list of behaviors. They are obvious enough not to require listing.

Table 3-1. Observable and measurable verbs.

Apply	Employ	Rank
Argue	Estimate	Rearrange
Assess	Examine	Recognize
Calculate	Explain	Record
Change	Express	Relate
Choose	Extrapolate	Repeat
Cite	Formulate	Rephrase
Classify	Identify	Report
Combine	Illustrate	Restate
Compare	Infer	Schedule
Conclude	Integrate	Score
Contrast	Interpolate	Sketch
Criticize	Interpret	Solve
Decide	Inventory	Specify
Define	Judge	Standardize
Derive	Manage	Tell
Design	Measure	Translate
Diagram	Name	Transmit
Differentiate	Operate	Underline
Discuss	Organize	Use
Dramatize	Prescribe	Validate
Draw up a list	Question	

Condition

The objectives in the earlier examples begin with the word "given." Objectives need to state the givens, or *conditions,* to ensure that learners have a complete and consistent foundation from which to work. The condition statement in an objective delineates the conditions for a given behavior. Conditions may include tangible things, like tools, books, equipment, or hardware; they may also have their basis in an instructional method. For example, a condition might read, "given a screwdriver and 10 screws" or "provided with a 1329A test set." Other less tangible conditions are "...following participation in a role play" or "...after having read chapter 4 of the text."

Although it may appear that condition statements are either too obvious to be useful or overly complicated, subtle differences in context can sink an otherwise great course. Some facilitators omit books or other reading material, or instructional methods intended for the course are replaced or eliminated based on a facilitator's whim. Failing to mention a specific book, other reading material, or an instructional method might seem insignificant, but it could result in a facilitator's taking a different approach to teaching. General condition statements, such as "when completed with this course," are inadequate because they do not provide any foundation from which to work. Try to be as thorough as possible in setting the context.

In the poison prevention course, for example, the conditions might be the following:

- given a planning sheet and sketch of a home or office
- after working with another participant in the course
- provided several real-life scenarios of potential poisoning hazards.

Each of these conditions provides a context that supports the other elements of an objective.

Degree

The *degree* statement is the instructional design equivalent to a price tag in retail: It sets the price. A learner will feel frustrated if he or she does not know what it takes to meet an objective.

Writing degree statements is like playing the game of horseshoes. The object of the game is to place the horseshoe's open end around a pole and get a set number of points. Players can also accumulate fewer points for being within a certain distance of the pole, usually the length of the horseshoe.

The object of learning is to meet an objective. A learner should be able to score some points even if he or she does not hit the mark. As instructional designers write their objectives, they need to be clear about how close a learner needs to get to meet them. The difficulty in writing degree statements is in the process of realistically setting the degree threshold. Some examples of degree statements are as follows:

- successfully three times
- without error
- within five minutes
- on three different models of the equipment
- by offering an opinion
- a learning contract
- a grade of 70 percent or better on the quiz
- five-minute speech on a topic of her choosing
- at least five baskets from the three-point line
- a rating of nine or above as scored by a panel of judges.

All of these degree statements meet the criterion of being a good objective element because they are observable and measurable. No doubt should exist in anyone's mind about what needs to be done to meet the objective.

The following degree statements come close but are not quite adequate:

- at the discretion of the instructor
- after participating
- at the end of the course.

Instructional designers should also be careful with statements that include such ambiguous words as "safely," "carefully," "honestly," and other adverbs. It is tough to avoid some of these words, but they require additional clarifying information if they are put in an objective. The word "safely," for example, would not be measurable in the phrase "use the machine safely" but would be measurable used this way: "...will be performed safely, as documented in the Occupational Safety and Health Administration (OSHA) 500 standards."

It is also necessary to use percentages carefully in degree statements. A passing grade of 85 percent or better on the final exam is fine as a degree. However, a cardiopulmonary resuscitation (CPR) class that says students will be able to perform CPR correctly 85 percent of the time would not be an acceptable threshold. For certain skill sets, anything less than 100 percent proficiency is of dubious value or wholly unacceptable.

Percentages must be reasonable. It is better to have an employee of a coffee shop meet an objective of making four acceptable lattes in a row, rather than one of operating the latte machine correctly at least 70 percent of the time.

Terminal and Enabling Objectives

Terminal objectives are the final behavioral outcomes of a specific instructional event. For a course on the safe handling of asbestos on a job site, a terminal objective might be as follows:

- Given a realistic scenario depicting the handling and disposal of asbestos at a work site, the participant in the asbestos supervisor's course should be able to supervise the work of at least two asbestos removal technicians. The participant must comply with all OSHA standards that relate to the specific situation depicted in the scenario. No deficiency will be allowed, and the participant must repeat the process until able to comply with the zero-deficiency standard.

This description clearly states the skill the participant should have at the end of the course. There can be as many terminal objectives as needed, whether one or a thousand. In large projects, instructional designers can end up with design plans that fit in a series of three-ring binders, but it is also possible to have just one. The number varies with the design needs.

Enabling objectives support the terminal objectives. In the asbestos example, the supervisor would have to perform all the tasks that will be taught. Following are two possible enabling objectives that show use of the equipment and tools of the asbestos technician:

- ■ Given a hammer and chisel and while suited, the technician should be able to remove sprayed asbestos from a wall or ceiling without being exposed to the asbestos dust.
- ■ Given a bag of asbestos materials collected on the work site, the technician should be able to dispose of the material in the removal containers without any leakage of material.

There are a number of different ways to write and format the two types of objectives. Terminal objectives have audience, behavior, condition, and degree components, but enabling objectives do not need the audience element. Some instructional designers insist that enabling objectives should read more like an evaluation task, as in the following example:

- ■ While wearing the proper clothing, the technician will use a hammer and chisel to remove asbestos safely.

How instructional designers write and format their objectives is up to them. Sometimes it is a good practice to combine elements of a terminal objective with those of an enabling objective to provide a much more readable format, as in the following example:

- ■ Given all required tools and safety equipment, the participant in the asbestos supervisor course should be able to:
  - — remove asbestos, without exposure, wearing proper safety equipment
  - — remove debris from the work site using the proper containers without any leakage of material.

It is important to be certain to have all the objectives in the proper order. In the previous example, the participant must wear the proper equipment before removing debris, so that objective comes first.

Objective Domains

Objective domains are categories of objectives that assist instructional designers in determining a number of important design elements. The four objective domains are cognitive, affective, psychomotor, and interpersonal. Primarily, they assist instructional designers in determining how to structure objectives, evaluations, and delivery systems. Designers seldom mix objectives and evaluation tasks from different objective domains because they may then lack validity.

Here's an example that demonstrates the importance of objective domains to designers without going into the science behind domains: An instructional designer who was working on a training program for technicians to repair a certain type of computer might use all four domains in the following way in the design process:

- *Cognitive domain:* A learner should be able to know how to repair the equipment set.
- *Psychomotor domain:* A learner should be able to physically remove cases and insert boards and should be able to perform other skills requiring the use of the body.
- *Affective domain:* Learners should be able to offer strategies to overcome negative feelings about repairing certain models.
- *Interpersonal domain:* Learners should be able to provide excellent customer service.

Following are descriptions of each domain in detail.

Cognitive Domain

The cognitive domain usually accounts for most of an instructional designer's objectives. Generally, the definition of *cognitive domain* in training is the cognitive, or thinking, actions of the brain that result from the act of processing sensory. The cognitive domain can be viewed as the output from a process. One could argue successfully that every objective has some component of the cognitive domain. The distinctions among domains become important because of overlaps like this. The output of the behavior is the point at which instructional designers can judge the predominant domain. For example, if the output from a behavior is mostly the processing of data, then the domain would be cognitive.

Following are examples of objectives in the cognitive domain:

- The learner should be able to distinguish circuit boards 14R and 17Y.
- The learner should be able to add and subtract fractions.
- The learner should be able to identify risk factors associated with hepatitis.
- The learner should be able to recite the organizational oath.

Psychomotor Domain

The *psychomotor domain* is undoubtedly the easiest one to identify. If an objective mainly requires movement, it is probably psychomotor. Learning to operate a machine and using a computer mouse are two examples of skills that are in the psychomotor domain. Although they both have some cognitive influence, they require movement for successful completion of the objective.

Here are some objectives for psychomotor behaviors:

- The learner should be able to change the toner cartridge in the copy machine.
- The learner should be able to assemble circuit pack 2349.
- The learner should be able to repair a broken antenna on a field radio.
- The learner should be able to attach option 7T to the main assembly.

Interpersonal Domain

Alex Romiszowski (1981) established the premise for the *interpersonal domain* in his publication "The How and Why of Performance Objectives." Although most instructional design literature pays far too little attention to this concept, it is a vital dimension to the objective domain concept and, in practice, offers the missing element that defines key objective sets that exist in the real world.

Many of the soft skill training programs in large organizations are in some way related to the interaction of two or more individuals. This is why interpersonal behaviors are important. Designers are often forced into serving as mediators in organizational disputes involving individuals or departments. Dealing with such interpersonal problems requires a separate objective set.

Examples of objectives involving interpersonal behaviors include the following:

- The learner should be able to identify an area of disagreement between the two departments.
- The learner should be able to answer the phone and take a message without displaying obvious anger or impatience.
- The learner should be able to participate in a role-play situation reflecting the key areas of conflict in the office.
- The learner should be able to answer a question without resorting to name-calling.

Affective Domain

Objectives in the *affective domain* are soft skills that are difficult to observe and measure. Constructing evaluation tasks for affective domains is difficult and may be the reason that some designers shy away from writing this objective.

Many instructional designers think it is nearly impossible to write a behavior statement for some affective domain objectives. Others argue that you cannot change the way someone "feels" about a subject. It is not easy, but it is usually possible to work effectively as a designer in these behaviors. The designer cannot work to change a learner's attitude, just the learner's behavior. For example, a training program on customer service for new clerks in a retail environment would have affective domain objectives. If the goal of the training is to influence behavior and not the interpersonal aspects of the issue (that is, how a clerk tells a customer that 32-inch jeans do not fit comfortably a 48-inch waist), an instructional designer would write objectives for affective domain behaviors.

An affective domain objective for this situation might be stated like this:

■ The learner in the New Clerks Training will describe at least two anger-displacement strategies in a case study situation involving a customer being aggressive about a return with no receipt.

The intent of this behavior statement is to get the new clerk to process the anger and maintain composure in this difficult situation, which the clerk will likely face on the job. It certainly is not the intent of the objective to keep the clerk from wanting to confront the customer.

Affective domain objectives and the issues associated with trying to operationalize the process will always be difficult. It can be very hard to separate behavior from the trigger that brings the response, and that is a challenge designers constantly face. Workplace violence is a good example of an affective domain issue.

A strategy for the training is to address individual worker's violent tendencies, and that involves affective domain. Helping supervisors deal with potentially violent workers before violence erupts addresses the interpersonal domain. Clearly, there are elements of all four domains at work in these examples. However, the focus is on one domain, whereas the others play an enabling role.

Following is how an objective might be written for the affective domain in the workplace violence example:

■ Given a stop-action role-play situation in which the Workplace Violence participant assumes the role of a worker who feels anger at another worker on the job, the participant should be able to successfully articulate at least two strategies to keep his or her anger under control when the role play stops for discussion.

Following is how an objective might be written for the interpersonal domain in the workplace violence example:

■ Given a role-play situation in which the Workplace Violence Prevention for Supervisors participant assumes the role of a supervisor who is facilitating a potentially violent workplace confrontation, the learner should be able to enact a strategy that prevents the situation from moving from confrontation to violence.

The difference in these two objectives is their focus. One approach intends to work within the emotional framework of the individual, whereas the other relies on interpersonal skills to diffuse a violent situation. Both have the same long-term goal of stopping violence, but they approach it in very different ways.

Using Objective Domains in the Design Process

Instructional designers should think about the following once they establish their primary objective domain:

- *Consistency throughout the design in domain-related areas:* These areas include performance agreement, materials, instructional methods, evaluation techniques, and any design elements that are influenced by domain. Crossing domains will disrupt the design and confuse or negate the objectives. For example, objectives written for a training program that instructs paramedics in the use of a defibrillator are probably going to be psychomotor. The designer's objectives and course design should stay largely in that domain. If the course ends up focusing on the emotional trauma associated with being a first responder, the designer has switched domains and endangered the original goal of the course, the use of a defibrillator.
- *Consistency with analysis data:* Designers should not cross domains when moving from analysis to design. They must not ignore analysis data by misreading the predominant domain. For example, in a course for paramedics, if the analysis data show that learners are worried about learning when and if to use the siren and lights on the ambulance, the topic of the final course should not focus on how to use specific brands and models of sirens and lights. Rather, the topic should be when-and-if concerns about the use of sirens and lights.

Degree of Difficulty

A number of taxonomies suggest that certain behaviors are more difficult to learn than others. For example, predicting is more difficult than defining, and distinguishing is less difficult than synthesizing.

A designer needs to know the *degrees of difficulty* to ensure that an objective follows a continuum from simple to complex or from easy to hard. Most learning theories suggest that moving a learner slowly up the slope of difficulty allows a gradual accumulation of information. People who are learning to play an instrument start with simple exercises to help them learn the basics. As they acquire more skill, they move to playing sequences of notes and then to playing short melodies.

As designers develop their objectives and evaluation tasks, they must keep in mind the degree of difficulty of single objectives and then the sequencing of all the objectives in a project. A good practice is to assign a numerical value for difficulty from

1 to 10 and then to rate each objective. The objectives should begin with the lower numbers and proceed to the higher. By following that sequence, it would be easy for designers to see if they have a problem in their sequencing.

In a course about running a marathon, for example, designers would sequence objectives in such a way that the less difficult skills or concepts are given in the beginning and the more difficult are offered at the end. For example, an early objective might be for a participant to take short, 1-mile runs every other day for a week. This objective is relatively easy compared with a terminal objective of running a 26-mile race and would probably rate a 1 or 2, whereas a series of 5-mile runs would rate a 4 or 5. The terminal objective of running 26 miles would rate the maximum (10) in this series because it is the most difficult objective in the course.

Evaluation Tasks and the Performance Agreement Principle

The usefulness of objectives is severely jeopardized without *evaluation tasks*. In fact, it makes little sense to bother with objectives if there is no intention to evaluate a learner's progress toward meeting them. Designers must develop the ability to construct evaluation tasks. The tasks must not be a hurdle in themselves; they must be achievable and based on real life.

Examples of simple evaluation tasks are as follows:

- Using the circuit pack labeled B-75, replace the defective processor board on the server and confirm that the server is operating without error.
- You have until 4:00 p.m. to correctly solve all 25 math problems.

Evaluation tasks are created during the design phase to ensure that every objective has a corresponding learner-level evaluation as part of the course. Every objective needs to have this evaluation to ensure performance agreement.

Performance Agreement Principle

Performance agreement is a design term that describes the process of matching objectives and evaluation tasks together in a curriculum. This is a key concept in ISD because it mandates that objectives always have an evaluation and that evaluations always have an objective.

One of the reasons that ISD is so useful is that it sticks to a process. The correct use of ISD makes it almost impossible to leave out major chunks of curriculum design. Performance agreement insists that instructional designers pay careful attention to balance in their design work by insisting on an evaluation of every objective.

As an example, here is an objective written for a segment of a course called Sales for the Beginner:

■ Given a realistic role-play situation with Sales for the Beginner, the learner playing the part of the salesperson should be able to present three reasons why the client should purchase a specific product.

With the objective written, the instructional designer will have to construct an evaluation task. Here is a suggested approach:

■ You have just entered the office of a major client. You have to make a case for buying your top-line product. It is important that you present at least three reasons why the client should purchase your product.

The designer would then have to measure the performance agreement. The behavior, condition, and degree statements are the key elements the designer would have to match in the objective and the evaluation task. The first step in determining performance agreement is to identify these three elements in each. Table 3-2 shows each element in the objective and the evaluation task. When all the behaviors, conditions, and degree statements agree, the designer has ensured performance agreement.

A good test of objectives is whether instructional designers are able to come up with an evaluation task. If it is not possible, the objective may be flawed in one or all of the three elements.

Correcting Performance Agreement Problems

The best way to fix problems with performance agreements is to change either the objective or the evaluation task to ensure the two are in agreement. Designers should

Table 3-2. The performance agreement match.

	Objective	Evaluation Task
Behavior	. . . the learner . . . should be able to present . . . reasons why the client should purchase a specific product	. . . you present . . . reasons why the client should purchase your product
Condition	Given a realistic role-play situation with . . . learner playing the part of the salesperson . . .	You have just entered the office of a major client. You have to make a case for buying your top-line product.
Degree	. . . present three reasons . . .	. . . three reasons . . .

base their decision about which to change on their analysis and the context of their course. Consider the following objective:

- Provided with a stethoscope and blood pressure measuring equipment, the Nursing 304 student should be able to determine the blood pressure of five patients, as verified by the instructor.

If the evaluation task and objective do not agree, the designer could change the evaluation task to have the student take the blood pressure of all the patients. Another possibility would be to change the objective to include making a determination of need and then measuring the blood pressure of only those patients that need to have it done.

Take a look at the following example:

- Given participation in a role-play situation, the Effective Intercultural Communications student should be able to say hello and good-bye in at least two languages other than English.

If the evaluation task and objective do not agree, the designer could change the objective from the requirement for hello and good-bye fluency to something else, or the designer could rewrite the evaluation task to have the student say hello in a large hotel lobby where numerous languages are being spoken.

In Conclusion

This chapter began the exploration of design. It covered the process of writing four-part objectives and explained how instructional designers use terminal and enabling objectives and the objective domains to make certain the objectives make sense. It explained how instructional designers adhere to the performance agreement principle to ensure they can assess the objectives.

The next chapter addresses the design of lesson plans, a crucial aspect of any instructional design project.

Putting What You Have Learned Into Action

Now, let's work through some exercises to build your confidence and start you on the road to designing a project of your own. Exercises 3-1 to 3-6 on the CD cover these topics:

- ✓ writing draft and process objectives
- ✓ determining audience, behavior, condition, and degree elements
- ✓ writing terminal and enabling objectives
- ✓ checking for performance agreement.

4 Design: The Nine Events of Instruction

Chapter Objectives

At the conclusion of this chapter, you should be able to

- describe the nine events of instruction
- provide examples of each of the nine events.

No doubt, you are familiar with the terms *instructor's guide, teaching guide, course plan,* or one of the other dozens of terms referring to a lesson plan. When combined with a design plan, you have the heart of instructional design deliverables.

Lesson plans are an integral component of most instructional design projects. The single most important reason is that training often requires implementation of the same course numerous times. It is essential that each implementation of the course is done in the same way to ensure conformance to content and quality standards.

Over the years, numerous designs for lesson plans have evolved. Although some designers claim that certain plans have their roots planted firmly in a theoretical base, most lesson plans are the product of honest efforts at finding a way to assist facilitators in implementing a course.

The Theory Behind It

The work of Gagne, Briggs, and Wager (1988) is the best source for background information on lesson plan design. One significant aspect of learning theory they describe is the formalization of approaches in designing training. The theory supports the notion that learners are more likely to retain the concepts, skills, and procedures taught to them if they are presented in a way that enhances and supports the way the mind works.

Researchers have been studying how the brain works for years and especially how it retains information. For instructional designers the "how" is an important question. The very essence of the designer's role is making sure that learners leave with demonstrated mastery of objectives. The *nine events of instruction* join theory and practice in a way that can be used in most design situations.

Gagne, Briggs, and Wager (1988) built the nine events of instruction on the work of other theorists who studied the way humans process information and move it from sensing to processing to storing in short- or long-term memory. The nine steps in this process and each so-called event have an instructional design component that is critical in lesson plan design. The nine events have application in lesson plans in ways beyond that of lecture and other traditional delivery modalities. Every training solution must be based on the way the learner processes information, or it just will not work. The nine events are universal in their importance to instructional design.

Here are the nine events of instruction in the author's and Gagne's terminology. To make the nine events more descriptive of their intent, the author has given them new, more literal titles (the terms in parentheses are Gagne's original names for each event):

1. gaining attention
2. direction (stating objectives)
3. recall (recall of prerequisite information)
4. content (presentation of new material)
5. application feedback—level 1 (guided learning)
6. application feedback—level 2 (eliciting performance)
7. application feedback—level 3 (feedback)
8. evaluation (assessment)
9. closure (retention and transfer).

Technology and the Nine Events

The nine events become even more important if designers are working on a project that is not a traditional facilitator-led course. Designers who use the nine events as the framework for this type of delivery system can be sure they will at least consider the ramifications of all these elements in their design.

It is important to remember that the nine-events approach to lesson plans is not always appropriate. The technology involved may not permit its use. It takes a great deal of work to build lesson plans this way. After designers use this approach for a while, though, they find that the thought process it stimulates becomes instinctive and that it helps them become better designers even if they never again build a lesson plan this way.

A Close Examination of the Nine Events

Descriptions of the nine events follow. Most of the events include an example that shows how to build a lesson plan using this approach. Exercises on the accompanying CD give you the chance to practice building your own lesson plan.

Gaining Attention

In the beginning of a course, it is necessary to help learners focus on the course. Sometimes *gaining attention* means setting a tone for the course, whereas other times it means turning off outside interference that is rumbling through a learner's mind. In all cases, the attention-gathering process needs to relate to the topic. A funny story or a joke is not a good attention-getting method as a rule because it can prove distracting, unless a facilitator is certain that it refers to the topic and presents it in a way that is not offensive to the learners.

Some of the methods for gaining attention that have proven effective include the following:

- playing video or audiotapes of one minute or less on the topic
- having a demonstration, such as modeling the task participants will learn in the course
- role playing, particularly for addressing affective and interpersonal domain objectives, such as sexual harassment and workplace violence.

Designers should not attempt to start a training program without knowing how the facilitators will gain participants' attention. The designers should let their imaginations go as they search for a way that will start their curricula off with an attention-getting bang.

Consider how a designer might use a video to gain participants' attention during a fictional safety course. (Note that this in no way is meant to be a real course. It is an example for lesson plans.) The course focuses on the increased risks of injury if proper safety procedures are not followed.

1. The designer says, "We are going to open our course with a short video highlighting the risks of injury that workers face in certain situations. The workers shown in the video are undoubtedly hard workers like all of us, but safety takes no holidays and this is a good example of what might happen."

2. Show the videotape—a one-minute depiction of an accident that injures several workers during routine work.

Nine Events Repackaged

It is also possible to take a more traditional approach to lesson design and arrange the nine events into three categories, which most people would view as a viable way to assemble a course. In that approach, the categories would follow this format:

A. Tell them what you are going to teach them.
1. Gaining attention
2. Direction
3. Recall
B. Teach them.
4. Content
5. Application feedback—level 1
6. Application feedback—level 2
7. Application feedback—level 3
8. Evaluation
C. Tell them what you taught them.
9. Closure (enhancing transfer).

3. Ask participants what they observed. The designer reiterates the video's point about using proper equipment and procedures.
4. The designer closes by saying, "I think we can all agree that following safety procedures are necessities for every worker's well-being. None of us wants to be injured or killed on the job."

Direction

The presentation of objectives is a crucial factor in determining the *direction* for meeting course objectives. Objectives set the destination so that learners will have a map that shows them where they're going.

Sometimes facilitators or designers say that they want learners to surmise the objectives or that the objectives should be a surprise. Some facilitators or designers ask learners what they would like to learn in a course. If there are any examples of instances in which these methods are successful, they are rare indeed! As chapter 3 described, objectives are the nucleus of all other aspects of instructional design.

Designers should state their objectives in a way that works for their audience. At this stage, they have already completed the audience analysis, which provides the direction for designing the objectives.

For the worker's safety lesson example, the designer needs to set the direction for the participants early in the course, just as any designer would with any project. Stating the objectives in the second event acts as a stabilizing force in your lesson plan. The designer would take the time to think through what it is he or she wants the learners to be able to do and what they should be able to do at the end of that particular session. Following is one approach the designer might take:

1. The designer might say something like the following: "The risks of injury on the job are a matter of life and death. They involve every one of us."
2. "Before you leave, you should be able to identify the potential risks of injury you face on the job."
3. "You should be able to demonstrate how to conduct checks for unsafe conditions."
4. "You should be able to describe how to report unsafe working conditions to a supervisor or union representative."

Recall

To set the context for the objectives, facilitators must prime the learners for the new material by following the three warm-up elements—that is, gaining attention, direction, and *recall*. It often takes a little bit of information to get learners thinking about the course content and objectives.

In some cases, the recall session may end up being technical to ensure the facilitator that participants are ready to move to the new material. Other times, it may be no more than a simple question or discussion that builds the foundation for the information that follows.

One design necessity of this prerequisite element is that it levels the playing field for the facilitator. Depending on content and course design, participants who lack the necessary competencies need assistance. A simple solution that works with some designs is to provide a simple handout or give a brief review. A more thorough review may be necessary if there is a large gap in knowledge or enough of the participants are having problems with the prerequisites.

Designers need to think through this aspect of their design. Effective designs build in options for the facilitators that allow them to add information as necessary once they determine a group's level of competency. For example, they could prepare to give participants handouts with prerequisite content as well as to hold a group discussion that covers the content. The discussion would work well in affective and interpersonal domain objectives.

Facilitators who find that one or more of the participants appear to be struggling with the prerequisite information could distribute a basic handout to provide them with a reference for the rest of the module. However, facilitators should be aware that such handouts, although they enlighten some, may bore others who are somewhat familiar with the subject matter and find prerequisite information as stimulating as reading yesterday's paper for the second time.

Facilitators who determine that one or more of the participants are competent enough to assist them with the class should sign them up for that role. They could have those participants circulate through the room, answering questions as necessary.

A pretest for review is a sound design practice. Instructional designers who are unsure of their population's entry competencies should screen potential participants before they attend a course, not after they arrive and expect to participate.

Content

How *content* is presented has more impact on learners than any other facet of the design. Implementation is about presenting new material in a way that ensures that learners meet objectives. Designers can be as creative as they wish just as long as they balance this creativity with what their analysis has told them about the learners.

Designers who are presenting highly technical training that resides predominantly in the cognitive domain need to strike a balance between mandated content and its numbing effect on the learners. They must find a way to make everything interesting. Their projects all will be different when it comes to content. They must use their imagination to its full advantage and choose presentation modalities that interest the learner and make the most of the resources available. Following is one example of how to do it, using mining as an example:

1. The instructor may say, "You know your job like the back of your hand, right? So tell me where the danger is in this picture?"
2. "All of the pictures you're about to see show areas where there were unsafe working conditions. Some of the problems are more obvious than others are. All the accidents were preventable. These pictures are also in your handouts."

Application Feedback—Level 1

Instructional designers like to use interactivity when building a course. It is almost as if they have an overwhelming need to allow and encourage participation by learners. The very word "participant" must have evolved from the notion of participation. To be effective, interactivity should not be a question tossed out into the room and batted around until something emerges. Designers need to shape and build momentum to keep learners engaged. *Application feedback* is the point at which designers can give the facilitator and learner an opportunity to begin practicing skills or discussing concepts critical to meeting lesson objectives.

In this first level of application feedback, it is essential that facilitator and learners share equally in the process. One excellent way to do this is to have a large group discussion that involves working though a problem or discussing a concept. It is important that the facilitator involve as many participants as possible in the discussion and draw in those who are holding back. Learners need to have a comfortable environment in which to ask questions. They also need to feel safe enough to experiment and ask a question that, in another environment, they may not ask for fear it would seem ridiculous.

Application Feedback—Level 2

Individual performance and practice in a safe environment are the main benefits of this event. Learners should now be able to test the waters of the new material. Generally, this portion of the training is built around small-group activities. It is important that learners have an opportunity both to offer and to receive information at this point.

Designers who want interactivity can make it happen during this stage. They should find ways to invite learners into the subject matter and also offer a low-level evaluation of the objective or objectives by both the facilitator and other learners. At this stage of the process, learners are largely on their own and receiving feedback from other learners and the facilitator.

By working in pairs or small groups, learners may ask questions of each other that they might not ask of a facilitator. Designers must provide an easy path from the small group to the facilitator so that learners who are unable to find an acceptable answer among themselves can go to the facilitator for answers and clarification as necessary.

Application Feedback—Level 3

It is really tough for people to make progress if they don't receive any information about how they are doing. This element serves as a learner's friend and partner in training. Avoiding this element produces weak training in both stand-up and technology-driven areas. No substitute exists for midcourse corrections in the learning process. A learner should not be allowed to get to the end of a training event without any information related to meeting the objectives.

First, designers must make sure through the objectives that each learner will get enough feedback about progress to allow correction of any uncertainty or error. A facilitator, another learner, or even a computer could deliver this information. The important thing is that it is delivered.

There are many ways to provide this feedback, and each design's specific objective domains, time limitations, level of difficulty of content, learner variables, and possibly other factors influence each designer's approach. One of the true tests of a good designer is how he or she determines the best feedback scheme for a given project.

In the safety example, course participants can review diagrams of their work areas to identify danger spots. A course like this demonstrates how important it is that learners meet objectives. An uncorrected mistake at this point may never get corrected and could eventually have life-threatening repercussions for the learner if an accident occurred.

Evaluation

If *evaluation* is one of the parents of instructional design, then evaluating performance is the first cousin. No learner should leave a training course without passing through an evaluation. This event doesn't always entail a test or other formal evaluation; it is usually just a check-off that ensures that the learner has met the objectives. But, every objective has to be evaluated or it isn't worth having as an objective. This is the basis of the performance agreement principle. Objectives have to match evaluation tasks, and it is tough to match these two if one is missing.

Evaluation needs to be a step above just providing feedback to the learner. It is easy to deliver the evaluation in designs that include a formal evaluation, such as a final test or certification exam. Designers need to find other ways of providing this feedback if they do not plan on offering an exam. For example, for a training program for a sales staff, designers might have a learner simulate closing a sale with a client. They can determine any remaining rough spots and provide the learner with any additional assistance needed to meet the project objectives.

There are several ways that designers could create the final evaluation for the safety class. One way would be for learners to describe to all members of the class the risks in their jobs and present a safety plan to reduce them. This provides one learner with an evaluation and the other learners with ideas that had not been presented before. Most important, the facilitator has the opportunity to comment on the learners' progress and correct any problems that remain.

Closure

During *closure,* instructional designers need to review the objectives and provide a recap for learners. It is important that learners appreciate the progress they have made and realize that they have met the objectives presented to them at the beginning of the course. The satisfaction of charting progress cannot be overstated. To accomplish these ends, designers have to provide the following during closure:

■ *Information about any course elements that follow:* Those elements might be the next course in a series or an optional add-on that is being offered. It is vital that the design provide a path to anything that follows. This path is not only for continuity, although it does provide that assistance, but also for prerequisite information so that learners know what to expect next. If they need to prepare any materials or read anything before attending the next course, they have the necessary information to do that.

■ *Generalizing information about the knowledge, skills, or abilities provided in the course:* If the content deals with learning to use a 2-quart pot for boiling potatoes, the facilitator might generalize by pointing out that the pot also works for making soup or by explaining two different ways to cook using the same pan. To take another example, in designing a course for attorneys about the communication skills for presenting opening arguments, a designer might generalize by showing that attorneys can also use that skill in closing arguments. At a communications level, only the words change, not the process of presenting.

■ *Synthesizing or finding ways to change the context of the learners' knowledge, skills, and abilities (KSAs):* This skill is to help learners find application of the objectives in a different frame of reference. In the pot example, synthesizing would mean using the pot for catching rainwater. In the attorney communication example, it might mean using that communication skill to argue for a refund at a department store. Synthesizing is important for expanding the dimension of the objectives. Once designers have moved the learner to the target objectives, they can really expand the value of the course.

In the safety example, learners might generalize by encouraging other staff members to look at photographs for dangers in their work areas and at home. The skill has not changed, but it is being generalized to include other areas where workers might confront safety issues. Changing the context of the objectives in this course might mean using a map of the learner's house and expanding it to include other danger zones. This is really using ISD to maximize the impact of the course.

Elimination of Events

Occasionally, designers choose to eliminate events. Sometimes there just isn't enough time for them to go through all of them. Other times nine events may be too complex for a particular project. When designing CBT or multimedia, it can be difficult to design the necessary feedback and interaction steps. Designers may then decide that they can reduce the nine events to seven or fewer events. Usually guided learning, eliciting performance, and feedback suffer the most in this environment.

Designers should be sure at least to consider all nine events when designing their course. Without this kind of guide for designing their lessons, they are likely to have an outline of the content and an instructional design with no structure, which is the cardinal sin of instructional design.

In Conclusion

This chapter finished the exploration of design. It describes the nine events of instruction, which are steps that guide instructors through the design of an effective lesson plan. The chapter also explained instances in which it may be necessary to reorder or eliminate some steps.

Putting What You Have Learned Into Action

Now, let's work through some exercises to build your confidence and start you on the road to designing a project of your own. The 13 exercises on the CD that correspond to this chapter cover these topics, which together comprise the nine events of instruction of a lesson plan:

1. gaining attention
2. direction
3. recall
4. content
5. application feedback—level 1
6. application feedback—level 2
7. application feedback—level 3
8. evaluation
9. closure.

Each exercise will give you an opportunity to practice the individual elements. If you are working on a project, use content from it as answers for the exercises. Otherwise, just use good ideas that will work for a number of different situations.

5 Development

Chapter Objectives

At the conclusion of this chapter, you should be able to

- define the development phase of ISD
- list several aspects of development that require reviewing when developing materials
- give several reasons why pilot testing is essential when designing a curriculum
- describe why a train-the-trainer course may be necessary
- list several things to consider when designing a train-the-trainer course.

The *development phase* of ISD is the period that connects the design process with the implementation of a project. Plans and prototypes move to realization as the designer moves materials to a final draft stage. Additionally, programmers code technology-based projects, and graphic artists produce artwork.

As the buffer between design and implementation, development necessitates that the instructional designer carefully monitor the process elements. It can be exciting for instructional designers to work with a variety of different professionals, but it can also be hectic. Careful communication at this point pays dividends later.

One of the most rewarding aspects of the development phase for instructional designers is that they get to see all of the design plans coming to life. Manuals, videos, webpages, and a hundred different tangible deliverables finally take shape. There is usually a collective sigh of relief once this happens, and it is easy to see why.

The development phase allows designers to put the finishing touches on the observable deliverables for a project. It is also the best opportunity to do pilot testing before a project goes into implementation.

Look and Feel

Development presents many opportunities to make mistakes in training design and production. Everyone has opinions about the way materials should appear, and it can sometimes be hard to get general agreement about even the simplest things. Designers play an important role in finding consensus and working with all elements of a project.

The process of moving from draft materials to a nearly final product is crucial to a project's success. Designers need to address any number of issues to ensure that the materials are satisfactory. Generally, they need to consider the following aspects of development when working on materials production:

- *Cost:* Designers must be sure they know what products are going to cost and that they stay on budget.
- *Deadlines:* They must set firm deadlines for production of materials and require that vendors stick to the deadlines.
- *Written agreements:* They must have everything in writing concerning paper, color, size, quantity, fonts, and other variables in their materials.
- *Samples:* They must always check a sample or proof of the materials before the production begins.
- *Final approval:* They must be sure to approve final copy of materials, not taking anyone's word for anything.
- *Pilot test:* Before producing the final materials, they must conduct pilot tests or have a review by stakeholders in the process, or do both. A pilot test evaluates the entire design, not just materials.

Pilot Testing

Pilot testing is a chance to evaluate a project before it goes into full implementation and is a key component of the development stage. The theory for instructional design is the same as that for a play: Both need rehearsals. It takes time to get all the bugs out of the implementation materials and lesson plans.

It is logical to pilot test before designers start producing final materials and begin the process of delivering their course. Some designers include pilot testing in the implementation phase, rather than in development, and that is fine. It is more important to test a project before finalizing deliverables than it is to worry about whether testing happens in the development or implementation phases.

Companies often view a pilot test, or pre-implementation practice session, as a luxury. Even if it is a luxury, that doesn't mean designers cannot expose their project to some scrutiny before moving it into implementation. At the very least, it can be useful to do a dry run with a colleague or a friend. Here are some things that designers should look for in a pilot test. If they detect any problems, they should correct them before finalizing that aspect of the program.

- Does the lesson plan work?
- Are the directions to the facilitator clear and concise?
- Are the facilitator's materials appropriate and thorough enough?
- Are the learner's materials appropriate and thorough enough?
- Are the support materials (slides, overheads, handouts, and the like) what you expected?
- Does the timing of each of the segments match your estimates?
- Are the technology components (audio, video, computers, and so forth) appropriate?
- Do the instructional methods work as planned?
- What does not work the way you thought it should?
- What needs to be changed?

During the review, designers should look for anything that doesn't seem to fit. Sometimes designers' instincts bring to their attention problems that may not be obvious to the subject matter experts or the client. It is this sixth sense about design that makes the role of the instructional designer so important.

Train-the-Trainer Courses

Another way to discover any problems is with a *train-the-trainer* (TTT) program, an often neglected aspect of instructional design. Like analysis, the process of providing this level of support for facilitators involves work and requires resources; in the end, however, the extra effort can make the difference between success and failure.

This critically important aspect of course implementation is often ignored for a variety of seemingly logical reasons. You've probably heard that TTT courses are not necessary because professional facilitators can take any course and implement it with a little practice. Another excuse is that there isn't any time or resources available to bring everyone together for the TTT process. A perennial favorite is the notion that any well-designed course (and all ISD courses are well designed, aren't they?) should not require any additional support for implementation.

As with every aspect of instructional design, the decision to require a TTT course is related to the rest of your course elements. If your system demands it, then you have to consider the ramifications of ignoring the warning. Here's a list of reasons for including a TTT element in instructional design:

■ new or unfamiliar content
■ new or unfamiliar delivery system
■ facilitator population with little or no previous facilitator experience
■ changes in content specifics that must be first taught to facilitators
■ new or unfamiliar technology demands on facilitators
■ online course management systems training specific to content
■ requirement that content be rigidly and uniformly implemented
■ licensure or certification required for facilitators.

A TTT course also provides the opportunity for pilot testing of a course, with the caution that the target population may not be in perfect sync with the design plan population profile. In some ways it may be a preferred method of piloting if the content must also be delivered to the facilitators. This is sometimes the case with mandated training or organization-wide rollouts. In this option, the training is often presented by the instructional design team, SMEs, or some combination of the two.

Train-the-Trainer Course Design

Several styles of TTT courses have evolved over the years, with most being some variation of the "see one, teach one" model. With this approach, facilitators first observe, or participate as learners, one implementation cycle of the course. They then facilitate all or some of the course content while being coached by both the design team and other facilitators. This approach works both in online and in-class settings.

There are many advantages to incorporating a complete observation cycle of the course in this model targeted toward future facilitators, including the fact that any questions facilitators have about the content can be addressed at the same time as issues associated with their implementation of the content.

The disadvantage of this approach is the time it takes to work through the process. In most cases it takes at least twice as long to implement the TTT course as the course actually takes in implementation to the intended population profile. That is why variations on this theme are becoming more focused on the unique aspects of a course and less on the actual art of facilitation, except in populations of novice facilitators.

Things to Consider in TTT Designs

As you work through the design of your TTT course, consider the following issues:

- To what degree does the population of facilitators require a facilitation skills upgrade or refresher?
- To what degree is the content new to the facilitators?
- Do you have any doubts about the ability of the facilitators to implement the course in areas that you can address in a TTT session?
- Are there any unique aspects of your course design or implementation that require facilitator participation in the content preparation (for example, field inclusion of data that the facilitator must gather and interpret)?

No matter what you decide concerning offering a TTT option, at least work through the advantages and disadvantages of your choice. As with most things in ISD, there is no one right or wrong answer.

In Conclusion

This chapter explored the development phase of ISD including the materials development process and the design of pilot testing and train-the-trainer programs.

Putting What You Have Learned Into Action

Exercises 5-1, 5-2, and 5-3 on the CD give you an opportunity to review the development phase of ISD.

6 Implementation

Chapter Objectives

At the conclusion of this chapter, you should be able to

- explain the implementation phase of the ISD process
- explain Donald Kirkpatrick's level 1 and 2 evaluation
- review the evaluation tasks associated with implementation.

Implementation is the ISD element that most nondesigners consider training and education. It is the time when learners sit in the classroom or in front of a computer for an online course. This phase connects the provider with the end user of the instruction; it is the most recognizable element of the ISD process.

It is axiomatic in project management that you are never more than 90 percent complete for any job on which you are working. It is the same with instructional design projects. It is time to move on to implementation if a designer has the basics covered, the pilot testing has gone well, and the designer has made the changes. Waiting for that next 10 percent improvement might take longer than the total time allocated for the project.

Not every designer implements the curricula he or she designs. In some cases, the designer never actually teaches the course or is a part of the learning technology solution he or she designed. This approach often is a good idea because designers who are also facilitators tend to believe that they can improvise a fix for missing or faulty design elements on the spot. Unfortunately, this usually is not the case. Making alterations on the fly is a real challenge, and facilitators are not always as experienced or capable of making a faulty lesson plan work as designers might want them to be. Nothing should be left to chance, especially if it allows a design to suffer in the hands of an inexperienced facilitator.

The evaluation of the implementation process must include an evaluation of learners' impressions of the training (that is, Kirkpatrick's level 1) and the validation of objectives being met by learners (that is, Kirkpatrick's level 2).

Kirkpatrick's Levels of Evaluation

Donald Kirkpatrick (1998) has broken evaluation into four levels that are easy to understand. Each of these has specific qualities and fits distinctive needs. Although these levels are linear, designers do not have to use them in any specific order to achieve their evaluation objectives. The *four levels of evaluation* are as follows:

- ■ level 1, reaction
- ■ level 2, learning
- ■ level 3, behavior
- ■ level 4, results.

This chapter includes descriptions of levels 1 and 2, which are essential ingredients of evaluation during implementation. Descriptions of levels 3 and 4 appear in chapter 7, which covers the evaluation phase of ADDIE.

Reaction, Level 1

Anyone who has ever completed an evaluation that asked for a *reaction* to a training course probably was responding to a level 1 evaluation. The most common evaluations at this level are smile sheets, which ask about likes and dislikes. Smile sheets are so common that some people use the term to refer to all evaluations at this level. Other level 1 evaluations are focus groups, which are held after training, and selective interviews in which people ask a sample of learners their opinions of training as they leave a program.

The aim of each of these level 1 evaluations is to discover learners' reactions to the process. More than anything, level 1 evaluation provides instant quality control data. ASTD reports that between 72 and 89 percent of organizations use level 1 evaluation (Bassi & Van Buren, 1999).

A good strategy for level 1 evaluation is to determine learners' initial responses to the experience as they exit the training. The freshest and most accurate data for a level 1 evaluation comes at the immediate conclusion of the training. Every minute that elapses from the end of the training to the reaction from a participant adds to the risk that inaccurate data will be collected. After all, designers are looking for a reaction. The sidebar lists some questions typically asked for level 1 evaluation of reaction.

Learning, Level 2

For instructional designers, evaluations at the learning level are tied directly to objectives, as you read in chapter 3 in the context of performance agreement. These are the evalu-

> **Examples of Level 1 Evaluation Questions**
>
> - Was your time well spent in this training?
> - Would you recommend this course to a co-worker?
> - What did you like best?
> - What did you like least?
> - Were the objectives made clear to you?
> - Do you feel you were able to meet the objectives?
> - Did you like the way the course was presented?
> - Was the room comfortable?
> - Is there anything you would like to tell us about the experience?

ation tasks that designers develop to match their objectives. Surprisingly, only 29 to 32 percent of organizations use a level 2 evaluation of *learning* (Bassi & Van Buren, 1999). This statistic indicates that less than a quarter of all training is evaluated in relationship to objectives, assuming there are any.

Performance agreement goes a long way toward ensuring that objectives are correctly evaluated. Chapter 3 described the following objective:

■ Given a realistic role-play situation with Sales for the Beginner, the learner playing the part of the salesperson should be able to present three reasons why the client should purchase a specific product.

With the objective in mind, the designer then generates an evaluation task:

■ You have just entered the office of a major client. You have to make a case for buying your top-line product. It is important that you present at least three reasons why the client should purchase your product.

The next step has the designer matching the key elements of behavior, condition, and degree in the objective and the evaluation task. Table 6-1 shows the key elements of performance agreement. The evaluation task column shows what Kirkpatrick calls level 2 evaluations.

Designers who follow the performance agreement principle of comparing the behavior and condition elements of both an objective and evaluation task will be accomplished level 2 designers.

Table 6-1. The performance agreement match.

	Objective	Evaluation Task
Behavior	. . . the learner . . . should be able to present . . . reasons why the client should purchase a specific product	. . . you present . . . reasons why the client should purchase your product
Condition	Given a realistic role-play situation with . . . learner playing the part of the salesperson . . .	You have just entered the office of a major client. You have to make a case for buying your top-line product.
Degree	. . . present three reasons . . .	. . . three reasons . . .

Other Elements of Evaluation

During implementation, other elements of evaluation must be present:

- evaluation from the perspective of the facilitator
- evaluation of the materials or technology
- evaluation of the environment (room size, arrangement)
- continuity and conformity of implementation with the design plan.

These elements are independent of the level process and have the potential for providing data that suggest changes are necessary. Every aspect of the design is subject to further alteration once implemented. As noted earlier, designers should never consider a project more than 90 percent complete. This means they have a work in progress, not a project that has no hope of redemption. Careful evaluation will provide ample opportunities for tweaks during and after implementation.

Even perfectionists can relax, knowing that everything is a work in progress, including content and materials. They may get the check in the mail for their work or be assigned to another project, but the designs they have worked on are still maturing.

In Conclusion

This chapter described the implementation phase, when participants encounter the instruction, and the importance of evaluation during this period. You learned about levels 1 and 2 of Kirkpatrick's levels of evaluation, which provide designers with information on participants' reactions to the training and on how well the learning meets the objectives.

Putting What You Have Learned Into Action

Now, let's work through some analysis exercises to build your confidence and start you on the road to designing a project of your own. Exercises 6-1 to 6-6 on the CD cover these topics:

- ✓ applying the elements of evaluation to implementation
- ✓ performing a level 1 evaluation
- ✓ performing a level 2 evaluation.

7 Evaluation

Chapter Objectives

At the conclusion of this chapter, you should be able to

- describe evaluation techniques for all five elements of the ADDIE model
- evaluate the four parts of an objective
- describe evaluation as it relates to the performance agreement principle
- list the four levels of evaluation, as described by Kirkpatrick
- design evaluation instruments for all four levels of evaluation.

Evaluating More Than Just Results

Evaluation is more than just a postcourse event. Evaluation takes place in every element of the ADDIE model. Designers even need to evaluate the evaluation process. This multidimensional approach to evaluation reflects ISD's systems approach to instructional design. Not only are the traditional evaluations reflected in learner performance and content mastery part of the design process, the ISD process itself is reviewed for conformance to best practice throughout the ADDIE elements.

Evaluation of the design process is just as important as a review of the content, and it is an essential part of a design strategy. If the same course receives positive content evaluations but negative process evaluations, there are probably design process problems with either the delivery system or the instructional methods and materials. Positive process evaluations but negative content evaluations from the same course point to such content problems as difficulty of objectives, performance agreement, or other areas related to the subject matter.

Evaluations during each of the other four ADDIE elements provide the quality control mechanism that ensures an honest and meaningful snapshot of both process and product. It is almost impossible for a project to be completed successfully without a comprehensive evaluation strategy that goes beyond looking at the issues associated with learners and facilitators; the process itself must be examined. Analysis, design, development, and implementation all have evaluation needs that designers should include in their projects.

Evaluation in the Analysis Phase

Evaluation in analysis centers on the notion that a project with a solid foundation should never stray too far from where it is designed to be. Even when issues arise that need serious attention, a designer's analysis, if done correctly, will provide the blueprint he or she needs to fine-tune problems later. This is not to say that an analysis stands forever, as an accurate analysis will tell a designer. The evaluation at this point is intended to just make sure that designers have a great starting point.

Evaluation in the Design Phase

Design-phase evaluation is critical to the success of a project. Designers have little chance for success if they allow a flawed instructional design to move forward to development and implementation. Objectives, evaluation tasks, and all the critical elements of course design take shape in the design phase, and they need to pass some level of evaluation. Evaluations here address problems early and, consequently, save time and money.

The value of design-phase evaluations is that they enable coordination of information among all those working on a project. For designers working on their own, it is important to have someone review their design phase work because it is easy for designers to lose focus when they become glued to the process. A quick evaluation of both product and process is an absolute necessity.

Information from even the best analysis can go astray in the hands of a technical writer or designer. A SME is the best resource to use to check that the content is correct and clear. A SME's review can prevent embarrassing errors from occurring when the course is rolled out.

ISD and Evaluation

To incorporate useful evaluation components during ISD, designers need to address certain questions; the responses to these questions will lead them to the things they'll need to evaluate for the program:

- Is this an issue or problem that can be completely fixed by training alone?
- Is this an issue or problem that can be improved by a training solution?
- Have you gathered all the data (enough data) concerning
  — population
  — subject matter
  — organizational goals
  — learner goals and needs
  — logistics
  — resources
  — constraints?
- Have you reviewed your analysis results with
  — stakeholders
  — SMEs
  — target population sample
  — other designers?
- Have you compared your findings against other internal or external benchmarks?
- Have you double-checked all of the above?

Designers need to ensure that the following evaluations take place:

- review of all the design plan elements by the SMEs and at least one other designer
- review of all objectives and evaluation tasks by the SMEs and at least one other designer
- review of evaluation strategy and materials
- review of all draft participant materials
- review of all draft facilitator materials
- review of all draft media
- review of everything by the decision makers
- sign-off by the manager or client on everything (if appropriate).

Evaluating Design Elements

The designer must incorporate evaluation components to assess the validity of the objectives and the extent to which the objectives correlate with the desired behavior and the process employed for learning-level (Kirkpatrick level 2) evaluation, that is, performance agreement. (See chapter 6 for details.)

Evaluating Objectives

The first step in the process is to identify each component in the objective. Following the recommendations made in other chapters, designers should scrutinize the four elements of a learning objective—audience, behavior, condition, and degree—and rate each element from 1 to 10 according to how well it is written.

Two examples follow. The first objective is not written well, and its evaluation shows where the problems exist. The second objective is much better and reflects good instructional design practice.

The first objective says:

■ At the end of this course, the learner will know about radar.

The components of the objective are as follows:

■ *audience:* the learner
■ *behavior:* will know about radar
■ *condition:* at the end of this course
■ *degree:* not available.

Here is a suggested rating:

■ 5 for the audience statement
■ 5 for behavior
■ 3 for condition
■ 0 for degree.

The designer would then calculate the quality of the objective. First, he or she would add the ratings for a total of 13, then divide by four to result in a number between 1 and 10. For this objective, the score is 3.25 out of a possible 10. It is not very good, but it gives an idea of what the course is about.

The next objective uses language more successfully:

■ Given four hours in the classroom and two hands-on exercises, the Radar 101 participant should be able to describe without error the five basic operational modes for a model R768 radar unit.
■ *audience:* the Radar 101 participant

■ *behavior:* should be able to describe the five basic operational modes for a model R768 radar unit

■ *condition:* given four hours in the classroom and two hands-on exercises

■ *degree:* without error.

The audience rates a 10 because it is not possible to have more information unless you name the students individually. The behaviors are a 10 because the objective states very clearly what the participant is expected to do. The condition is a little weak because it could include materials, so give it an 8. The degree is clear enough to deserve a 10. The score on this objective is 9.5, much better than the first objective's score of 3.25.

This use of a 1-10 rating system may appear subjective, but a system can be developed that will apply to different designs and provide great value to the evaluation process.

Degree of Difficulty of Objectives

The term *degree of difficulty* does not refer to how difficult objectives are to write but how difficult they are for the learner to meet. An evaluation is important regardless of the complexity or age group with which a designer is working. There are several reasons designers are concerned about difficulty. First, the level of difficulty in a series of objectives ensures placement from easy to hard in the design. The level may not be obvious unless the designer rates the objectives. Second, designers need to be aware of difficulty to ensure themselves that they are challenging their learners at the level at which their analysis shows the learners can both absorb and synthesize. Third, if they are evaluating another project, they need to make sure that the level and sequencing of objectives are consistent with the project's goals.

Designers use the verb in each behavior for rating the difficulty because it is the heart of the objective. The verb shows that the designer is asking a participant to do "something" and that something is associated with a particular level of difficulty. Designers should rate the difficulty the same as they do the objectives, using a scale from 1 to 10. Consider, for example, ratings for the following action verbs:

■ "List" is not very difficult, so it will be a 3.

■ "Apply" is more difficult and deserves a 5.

■ "Criticize" is a 10 because it is more difficult than the first two.

(These ratings are just an example because there are contexts in which a designer may classify "apply" or "criticize" as less difficult than "list." Subtle differences between items, for example, may make it hard to list them in certain orders, a lesson may be so clear that it is easy to apply it, or the merits and demerits of certain items may be so obvious that criticism comes easily.)

If these three behavior verbs were in one module, a designer would want to order them from easy to hard. There are exceptions, such as when a designer wants to start with a more difficult concept or skill and then move to easier objectives. But, use your design skills to write and sequence your objectives according to their level of difficulty.

Performance Agreement

Performance agreement is the relationship between behavior and condition elements in objectives and evaluation tasks. The link between the two is critical to ensuring that the performance stated in the objective is in agreement with the performance in the evaluation task. Performance agreement is comparable to motion pictures in that one of the most important jobs on a movie set is that known as continuity. The person who handles continuity makes sure the filming matches the script and ensures that the sequence of the final product matches the script.

Similarly, the designer must make sure that objectives are written correctly and that the evaluation task supports the objective in behavior and degree. The designer facilitates this process by checking performance agreement.

Following is an example of an objective and its evaluation task:

- *Objective:* Given a car and a filling station, the Fueling the Car participant will fill the car without spilling any gas.
- *Evaluation task:* You have just stopped at a filling station. Fill the car completely without spilling any gas.

This example illustrates performance agreement, as table 7-1 shows. The behaviors, conditions, and evaluation task match.

Following is an example without performance agreement:

- *Objective:* An intern working with a doctor at the hospital in the Internal Medicine Rounds program should be able to perform CPR on a patient during a code blue emergency.

Table 7-1. The performance agreement match, example 1.

	Objective	Evaluation Task
Behavior	will fill the car	fill the car
Condition	given a car and a filling station	you have just stopped at a filling station

■ *Evaluation task:* You are performing rounds with your assigned doctor when a "code blue" is called in the next room. The nurse calls out that it appears to be a heart attack. You and the lead physician hurry to the room and determine that it is, in fact, a patient with no pulse. The lead physician orders you to perform CPR while he finds the defibrillator. In 500 words, describe how you would perform CPR.

Here the behavior in the objective and the evaluation task do not agree, as table 7-2 shows. The conditions match, but *performing* and *describing* are two vastly different behaviors. In this case, the mismatch could prove life threatening.

To fix this missing agreement, the designer could either rewrite the objective so that the behavior says, "should be able to describe" or change the evaluation task to say, "perform CPR on the patient."

It is a good idea to check performance agreement for all of your objectives, even if the consequences are not life threatening.

Evaluation in the Development Phase

Evaluation is also important in this phase, when many critical decisions are made that can greatly affect the success of your project. Designers must make sure their evaluation plan is ready for the pilot testing of the project. Issues that typically come up as they pilot test are segment timing, deficiencies in materials, lack of clarity in the course structure, and failure to design for the target population. A dozen other minor things may arise as well.

Segment timing is sometimes the hardest task for a designer. Differences in facilitators, equipment, and materials affect timing. A designer should allow for the possibility that any variable may affect timing. It is usually a good design strategy to add extra time. It is also valuable to time several run-throughs of a segment and average the time for the design. It is fairly common to find *deficiencies in materials* during pilot testing. These problems can range from typographic errors in the copy to offensive graphics or wording. Sometimes simple issues, such as having the

Table 7-2. The performance agreement match, example 2.

	Objective	Evaluation Task
Behavior	perform CPR on a patient	describe how you would perform CPR
Condition	working with a doctor at the hospital	performing rounds with your assigned doctor

materials in the right language, come into play. Just when a designer thinks everything is under control, someone will notice a problem in the materials, perhaps an error in the chief executive officer's name. Designers should fix all errors.

Clarity in the structure of a course is essential if the course is to be effective. Designers do not devote weeks and months to preparing a course just to watch facilitators struggle with the flow of the course or the participants roll their eyes skyward. Pilot tests often reveal holes in the population analysis, indicating that it undershot or overshot the average learner. It is the designer's responsibility to adjust the population information and content to match the pilot test's findings.

Evaluation in the Implementation Phase

The traditional approach to evaluation during implementation is the use of smile sheets, which show the reaction or response of the learner to the experience. Although these evaluations are an important part of a great evaluation strategy, they are only one small part of what a designer needs to do. Evaluation in this phase needs to cover every aspect of the interaction between the product and the end user.

Table 7-3 shows some components of evaluations during the implementation phase from the perspective of various stakeholders.

Evaluation in the Evaluation Phase

Designers who have evaluated everything in the other four phases will probably find that the evaluation phase is the easiest part of the evaluations. Evaluation products that designers complete during the evaluation phase may include project-end reviews and program evaluations for grants. Each of these is important and requires designers to do some thoughtful retrospection of both process and product for the project.

Table 7-3. Components of evaluations.

Learner	Facilitator	Client	Instructional Designer
Reaction	Reaction	Reaction	Objectives
Accomplishment	Usefulness	Value	Performance
Valuing	Content	Effectiveness	agreement
Investment	Presentation		Content
Reality	Process		Quality
	Reality		Timing
			Participants, clients,
			and facilitators
			Reality

Project-end reviews have two purposes. First, they look at how well the process worked for delivering the project. Designers should conduct these reviews whether they are working alone or have 30 staff members. To arrive at some objective data, it is important that each person involved reflects on what happened and share those observations with the other people involved. If the training was contentious, it is best for the people involved to gather the initial feedback anonymously because participants may not want to give honest evaluations if they fear reprisals for their answers. Later, the designer can bring everyone together and work through the problems. If the problems are not fixed at the evaluation stage, they are doomed to be repeated.

Grants usually require program evaluations because the groups that give money want to know what they got for it. These evaluations give designers an opportunity to highlight the best part of the project.

Evaluation data, when presented with graphs or other visual elements, make the case for success. Designers should review the objectives and course rationale and then ensure that the evaluation underscores the results that support those goals.

More on Kirkpatrick's Levels of Evaluation

This book has made clear the importance of including evaluation through all stages of design and implementation of training. Chapter 6 explained the first two levels of Kirkpatrick's four levels of evaluation. Level 1 is reaction, during which participants tell what they liked and disliked about the training program; and level 2 is learning, during which designers assess whether participants met the objectives. Levels 3 and 4, behavior and results, take place following training. Explanations of levels 3 and 4 follow.

Behavior, Level 3

Posttraining evaluation is a level 3 evaluation. The most important question it seeks to answer is, "Did the training stick?" How much of the training transferred from delivery to the workplace? Between 11 and 12 percent of training is evaluated for behavioral change (Bassi & Van Buren, 1999). This statistic means that just one training project out of 10 is evaluated for effectiveness.

There are a number of ways to conduct level 3 evaluations so that any designer can add this level to a tool kit. Surveys and observation are two powerful ways to evaluate at this level. The thing to remember about this level of evaluation is the behavior. Did the behavior move to the workplace? If designers' objectives are written well, they have half of what they need. The other half is to select a way to measure where participants start and where they are when designers measure long-term results.

Designers who are interested in seeing if participants can meet the training objectives will evaluate learning, whereas those who are interested in seeing if performance has improved will measure behavior. Both of these can be satisfied with evaluation.

For example, evaluations would differ for a course on the use of new software for entering orders in a retail sales environment. A designer is interested in finding out if the course had any impact. Accurate data is available on how long it took to complete a transaction before the training with both the new and old software. At regular intervals, the designer accumulates new data on how long it takes to complete a transaction and compares the numbers. The designer can easily detect any difference in time to see if the training had any impact and how much of an impact.

Designers who want to find out how much of the training objectives learners can still meet can sample a representative number of participants using the formal evaluation task used during the course. They then compare the scores on an individual or group basis and do the math. This method will go a long way toward evaluating if the content, as well as the instructional and delivery methods, were the best choices for the project.

In situations in which the evaluation is not so simple (with soft skills or affective domain courses, for example), designers can interview or survey participants and gauge the participants' opinion of their ability to still meet the objectives. If possible, designers can also retest a sampling of the participants.

There are three basic reasons why participants may lose the ability to meet objectives after the course, each of which tells the designer something important about the course. The reasons are covered in detail here.

Participants Never Learned the Skill or Concept. If participants never learned the content, the designer may have a breakdown in the level 3 evaluation of the course objectives. Having a large number of participants in this category usually indicates errors in implementation or design. Designers must carefully evaluate the course design and pay special attention to the population information.

It is possible that the facilitators who carried out the implementation may have done a poor job or didn't follow the lesson plan as provided. It might be that the participants ignored the prerequisites for the program. It is also possible that the evaluation tasks were either ignored or compromised to the point that participants were never evaluated at all. The lack of an evaluation sets up a scenario in which neither participant nor facilitator can really tell if the objectives are being met.

Design flaws could be as simple as poor performance agreement or disregard for a lesson plan structure that supports acquisition of content. Motivation and attitude are also concerns when objectives are not being met across the sample participant pool.

The Skill or Concept Was Never Retained. Problems with retention may come from any number of issues. The most common problems are too much content in too short a time or a lack of any supportive materials or methods after the conclusion of the course. It is also possible that the content had no meaning or importance to the participant. Ownership of the content is important if participants are to retain information for any length of time. Ownership necessarily implies content and course design that allows that to happen.

The Skill or Concept Was Never Used After the Course. Designers who determine that participants had no opportunity to use the skills or concepts sometimes face issues beyond their control. They may train 300 women and men to be motorcycle mechanics, but if nearly all of them end up in sales, the training will not stick. These kinds of issues are especially important in psychomotor and cognitive objective domains. Yes, people may be able to ride a bike after many years of no practice, but how many years of practice have they had to support those skills?

Results, Level 4

A level 4 evaluation is about results—bottom-line results. Kirkpatrick (1998) offers these examples of results that can be measured at level 4: "reduction of costs; reduction of turnover and absenteeism; reduction of grievances; increase in quality and quantity or production; or improved morale which, it is hoped, will lead to some of the previously stated results." Stated otherwise, did the training pay off? Were the expected or promised results accomplished?

This level of evaluation has also drawn more than a few skeptics because inflated claims of results, sometimes measured as return-on-investment (ROI), have sometimes entered into the process and driven many to question any "claimed" results.

Probably less than 3 percent of training is evaluated for results (Bassi & Van Buren, 1999). Make no mistake about it: Figuring results can be a tricky and sometimes expensive undertaking. One reason for this is that the value of results can be both monetary and societal in nature. Although the impact on an organization can be calculated with some degree of certainty, the impact on a community is tough to measure and is largely subjective in nature.

However, no one should discount the power that training can have for change in a community. The poison prevention course, for example, is community based, and the impact could be lifesaving in a very literal sense—a true level 4 result.

In Conclusion

This chapter completes the description of the five elements of the ADDIE model. It showed that the final element, evaluation, must be an integral part of all the other elements. The chapter also concluded the description of Kirkpatrick's four levels of evaluation.

Putting What You Have Learned Into Action

Now, let's work through some exercises to build your confidence and start you on the road to designing a project of your own. Exercises 7-1, 7-2, and 7-3 on the CD cover these topics:

✓   performing a level 3 evaluation.
✓   performing a level 4 evaluation.

Section 3　The Basics of the Design and Lesson Plans

8 Design Plan

Chapter Objectives

At the conclusion of this chapter, you should be able to

- describe the elements of a design plan
- construct a design plan.

This chapter gives readers the opportunity to assemble one of the two major components of quality instructional design—the design plan. The design plan serves as the anchor for the entire instructional design process. Once readers have mastered the individual elements of a design plan, they have the skills necessary to develop one for any project they work on in the future. The poison prevention course provides readers with a model.

The Design Plan

The process of designing an instructional program goes beyond delivering the training. Although most observers consider implementation the most perceptible part of the process, it just touches the surface of the designer's work. Even a great musician rarely just picks up an instrument and plays a song well the first time. Musicians spend a great deal of time working so that the notes their audience hears come to life. The concept is similar for a design project.

Most learners, and others outside the design process, see only the facilitator and the other learners. They are seldom aware of the hours, days, or months that went into the project from the design perspective. This is where a *design plan* comes into place. Before, during, and after the observable aspects of the training are implemented, the designer's work is documented in a package of design elements that outlines the basics of the project from the ISD perspective.

A design plan is also the detailed explanation that every project should have to be complete. Designers who cannot answer all the questions raised in a design plan may need to spend more time reviewing each element to ensure that they have a well-designed project.

Following are some important elements to include in a design plan:

- rationale
- target population
- description
- objectives
- evaluation strategy
- participant prerequisites
- facilitator prerequisites
- deliverables.

A description of each of these elements follows. Designers may come up with other things that are important for their project, and they should add or subtract sections as their projects demand. Nevertheless, it is best to include them all to ensure a complete design plan that covers all the bases. For example, designers in the training or education department of an organization may feel that facilitator prerequisites are unnecessary because the facilitators are known, and so they may leave them out of the design plan. There is no right or wrong when if comes to what is included. The important point is that designers have a design plan and that it covers any elements necessary to explain the project fully.

Rationale

A *rationale* is the mission statement for the project. A designer who can capsulize his or her project into a short, tightly written narrative has several important pieces of information about the effort and can communicate them to others. First, that designer knows where the project is going. Second, the designer knows how to get there. Third, the designer knows why it is important to go there in the first place. The rationale is comparable to a lawyer's opening statement.

A typical rationale is several paragraphs to several pages long. It should not be a word longer than it needs to be or a word shorter than is necessary to make the case for the project. Designers have to make sure they have a mission statement mentality as they write the rationale. In other words, they should make their points as if they were writing a mission statement for the project. Designers should let their cerebral side come to the surface as they compose a rationale for the project.

The rationale needs to answer several central questions:

- What are the reasons for having the course?
- What population or populations does it serve?
- Who is sponsoring the course?
- What is unique about it?
- Why should anyone participate as a learner or sponsor?

A rationale for the model poison prevention course is worded like this:

Accidental poisonings in the home are a horrifying fact of life in too many families. All it takes to set the scene for this tragedy is for someone to have a short lapse of memory during which the person forgets to close a cabinet door or a container of prescription medication. Those openings can be invitations to a curious child. Accidental poisonings can be easily prevented by implementation of some simple steps. The Poison Prevention in the Home course is designed to provide a quick, powerful lesson in poison prevention for any concerned adult.

Sponsored by a national health-care provider, this course offers a unique method of identifying potential poisoning hazards. Participants draw a map of their residence and highlight the areas that represent poisoning hot spots. Participants make a list of poisons in that location and complete a plan of action for dealing with any hazards. Because poisonings do not always occur in conveniently marked locations around the house, the course employs a secondary strategy for identifying hazards not usually associated with a specific room. Participants then list these hazards and develop a strategy to address those poisons.

This course is implemented in less than 90 minutes, with actual course time set at 60 minutes. The additional 30 minutes are for housekeeping items and a question-and-answer session after the formal class. To allow participant interaction, the anticipated class size is 25 or fewer for each offering.

Handouts, a videotape, and computer-based slides will be provided for each facilitator. A train-the-trainer session will be required for each facilitator before he or she will be certified to implement the course. The target population for this course is adults with an interest in preventing poisoning in their homes.

Target Population

For the design and the learners to resonate together in a project, designers need to define the *target population* or *end user*. The description does not have to be a long narrative, but it should cover all the bases. Although everyone involved in a project should be aware of its target population, people still make surprising assumptions about who will attend their courses. Some of these assumptions may be so irrelevant for the true population of the course that, if not corrected, they could ruin any chance that a design could work. For a course in a technical area, for example, designers once assumed that their audience would include newly hired, entry-level personnel as well as seasoned veteran technicians or supervisors. Unless these designers refined the target population early in the process, they would have wasted valuable resources of time and money either by implementing the course to the wrong population or redesigning it at a point that required making major revisions of content and techniques. To avoid such a lose-lose proposition, it is important to focus on the target population section of the design plan.

The target population statement must include those aspects of the population that can cause problems from a design perspective. Too much detail is clutter that should be avoided. It is not necessary to hinge design decisions on population elements such as gender and age if they will not affect course content. Designers should just stick to the facts that illustrate the population and have the potential to cause them problems.

As designers begin to write the target population section of the design plan, they should close their eyes and picture the audience waiting for the course to begin. If they cannot give a detailed description of that group, they have either a design problem to solve or an open-enrollment situation. Designers should picture a group of people slowly emerging from a dense fog and, as they get closer, begin to add details to what they are viewing. Then, they should write down what they see and add as much detail as the situation demands. In some instructional designs, the population overview can become complex.

Following is a description of the target population of the poison prevention course:

> This population is largely adults with a high-school education and an interest in preventing accidental poisoning in their homes. This group will be self-motivated to attend based on the marketing strategy employed by the course sponsor.

Description

The *description* section of the design plan paints a picture of the project that describes the structure of the training. Common elements to consider for the course description are as follows:

- ■ total course length
- ■ module length (if appropriate)
- ■ instructional method
- ■ materials.

For the poison prevention model course, a description looks like this:

The poison prevention training is structured and lasts 60 minutes. Instructional methodologies employed include lecture, small group activities, and learner presentation and discussions. The room must be compliant with the Americans with Disabilities Act (ADA) and have the capacity to provide computer projection. Recommended class size is 25 or fewer unless an assistant is available.

Designers must make sure their course description provides enough detail to depict the design of the project—accurately.

Objectives

The foundation and direction of the design plan are set under *objectives,* and everything else builds from them. All the terminal objectives go in this section. At times, the number of objectives may be so large that a designer must list them in an appendix or elsewhere for easy reference. Large projects can easily have hundreds of objectives.

The poison prevention course has the following objective:

- Given handouts, a job aid, and class discussion, the Poison Prevention in the Home participant should be able to create a plan to store poisons that eliminates any chance that children or pets can gain access to a poison.

Evaluation Strategy

In the *evaluation strategy* part of the design plan, designers explain their thoughts behind the evaluation plan; they do not give examples of evaluation tasks.

The evaluation strategy for the poison prevention course is rather simple. It depends on participants working with others in the class while the facilitator moves through the course checking on each participant. The description in the design plan might look like this:

> This course will use a level 2 peer-to-peer evaluation strategy supported by a facilitator's observations. With an open enrollment group this large (25 or so), it is unrealistic to expect to implement a more formal evaluation strategy. Given the time limitation (one hour) and instructional methods, it is necessary to rely on peer interaction to provide the first evaluation and on the facilitator to provide secondary evaluative support. It is anticipated that participants should be able to meet the course objective evaluated with this strategy.
>
> The evaluation will take place at the end of the course when each participant is expected to draw a map of his or her house and identify possible poison danger spots. Working with a peer, each participant will complete his or her map and show it to a partner. Each partner will offer advice and comments for improvement. The facilitator will answer questions as he or she visits each group.
>
> Participants will complete a level 1 evaluation to measure their reactions to the course and the training room environment.

The design need not go further than the foregoing description to ensure that there is a thorough overview of the evaluation process.

Participant Prerequisites

It is an absolute necessity that participants meet any *prerequisites* for a course they are slated to attend. This gatekeeper process describes entry-level competencies that are necessary to prevent population mismatches in courses. The analysis element of the ADDIE model provides this information about what the prerequisites should be.

Designers have to accept the fact that their prerequisites are not always honored. It is not unusual to see an instructor provide training at a lower level to meet the needs of the lowest common denominator in the target population.

Designers can use a tool known as *ranging* to widen the gate for a course without throwing the prerequisites away. When they apply ranging, they are setting the highest and lowest points of entry for participation in the course. They would specify these points in their design.

An example will illustrate how ranging works. Consider a designer who is working on a new word-processing program. An organization is standardizing its software and upgrading it at the same time. There are a number of objectives for the four-hour course, and most require prior knowledge of the software's previous version. The dilemma is that many people in the target population have no experience with the software because they have been using a different program in their department.

The designer realizes that the new software is not that much different from the software other departments have been using. For the training course, the designer decides to remove some of the more advanced features of the software and provide a general overview of the new software. The prerequisite section of the design plan for the course might read thus:

■ Participants must have at least six months' experience with any word-processing software that includes mail-merge and label-making applications. Participants with less experience will be required to complete the Basic Features tutorial for the new software before attending the course.

Ranging lets designers establish reasonable prerequisites for participants and still provide a path for the learners who cannot meet them. This example showed how ranging would accommodate low-prerequisite learners. Ranging also accommodates overqualified learners.

In the software training example, a small group within the target population has learned the new software on its own. This group does not need the training but does need the certificate to qualify for an upgrade. Ranging can accommodate that population by adding the following sentence to the prerequisite description:

■ Participants with prior experience on the software have the option of completing a short evaluation to receive the course certificate.

The design plan would identify the following prerequisites for participants:

■ Participants must have at least six months' experience with any word-processing software that includes mail-merge and label-making applications. Participants with less experience will be required to complete the Basic Features tutorial for the new software before attending the course. Participants with prior experience on the software have the option of completing a short evaluation to receive the course certificate.

Ranging works well in most situations, although it should not be applied in projects that require a very high level of entrance competencies or prior certification. In these cases the level of skills necessary at entry are fixed by the demands of the course.

The poison prevention class would have a different type of participant prerequisite description than the software class. Because it has open enrollment, the poison prevention course would have very general prerequisites so as to include many different types of people. The course description might read as follows:

■ Participants should have an interest in poison prevention and a willingness to participate in small group situations. The course will be delivered in English and requires some basic writing skills at the high-school level.

Facilitator Prerequisites

Anyone who has ever attended a course that was facilitated by someone who did not have any substantial knowledge of the subject matter knows how important it is to ensure that facilitators meet certain specifications. These *prerequisites* allow designers to prepare lesson plans and other materials knowing that facilitators meet a necessary skill level. Designers who add this information to their design plan move their work up a notch in terms of design skills. The specification for the software class might state:

■ The facilitator must have attended an advanced course in the software and received certification as a facilitator.

For the poison prevention course, the prerequisites for facilitators state:

■ The facilitator must have attended the four-hour train-the-trainer program sponsored by the course provider. Those unable to attend the train-the-trainer course may qualify as a facilitator by attending and serving as an assistant facilitator for a minimum of four course presentations.

The foregoing example shows that ranging also works for facilitators. By providing an entryway for potential facilitators who did not attend the train-the-trainer program, the designer has provided a second path by which to meet the qualifications.

Deliverables

In the last section of the design plan, designers specify everything that will be delivered as part of the project. *Deliverables* are usually tangibles like analytical reports, draft materials, courses on software or other technologies, evaluation forms, and even the design plan itself.

The design plan would specify the following deliverables for the poison prevention course, for example:

- analysis report
- design plan
- draft version of the facilitator's guide
- draft participant handouts and information sheets
- draft evaluation instruments
- final camera-ready copies of all draft materials
- project evaluation.

In Conclusion

This chapter explained that the design plan is the detailed description of every aspect of a design project. Plans typically include each of the following elements:

- rationale
- target population
- description
- objectives
- evaluation strategy
- participant prerequisites
- facilitator prerequisites
- deliverables.

The chapter defined each of the elements and included examples of how a designer might explain each one in a design plan.

Putting What You Have Learned Into Action

Exercises 8-1 and 8-2 on the CD give you an opportunity to review a completed design plan and complete one for your own course. They cover each topic in the design plan.

9 Lesson Plan

Chapter Objectives

At the conclusion of this chapter, you should be able to

- name the elements of a lesson plan
- construct a lesson plan.

In the last chapter, you learned the steps involved in creating your design plan, the first of two important ISD elements. This chapter gives you the opportunity to complete the second element—the lesson plan. By working from the design plan completed in the previous chapter, you will be able to create a finished design project worthy of implementation. The exercises on the CD pertaining to this chapter provide you with a template from which to build your own lesson plan.

The Facilitator

Facilitators are the key variable in any instructional design project. A facilitator may also be called a teacher, lecturer, discussion leader, professor, or any of a hundred different titles for the same function depending on the environment and practice within a learning environment. Facilitation also exists in distance learning and other distributed learning systems. The main factor to remember as an instructional designer is that facilitators need the right tools to make your design come to life and be successfully implemented. The more you provide a facilitator in terms of your lesson plan, the more likely it is that the facilitator will be successful.

For example, no one likes to get lost while driving. In many people, getting lost evokes feelings of aggravation and stress, and those feelings are only intensified if they are also late. Designers should keep this in mind when they are working on a training project. If they fail to offer facilitators all the information they need to implement the project, they will get lost. The stress associated with facilitating a misdirected training course can have disastrous effects on both the facilitator and the participants.

It is sometimes worse to get skimpy directions than none at all. Right now, a distressed trainer is sitting over coffee somewhere wondering how to deliver an eight-hour course from two pages of an outline.

The facilitator is as vital to the success of a design project as any other element. The more information designers can provide facilitators, the more likely they are to succeed. Lesson plans must be complete enough to allow anyone with the necessary subject matter experience to lead the course.

One of the first things designers need to consider as they approach the lesson plan stage of their design work is who their facilitators are. They should consider the following:

- Can the designer identify a range of experience within the pool of potential facilitators?
- Are there any special issues the designer needs to address, such as language or culture concerns? Will the facilitators require materials in a second language? Does the lesson plan allow facilitators to lead the course in a culturally appropriate way?

The information about the facilitators should appear in the design plan because it aids in the development of the lesson plan.

The Format of the Lesson Plan

Every lesson plan needs to have a *format* that lends itself to making the implementation of the course as simple as possible. Designers need to use a consistent format if there will be a series of courses. Some stylistic elements that allow for an easy transition from one course to the next include the ideas presented in the following sections. A completed lesson plan is included on the accompanying CD.

Nine Events of Instruction

Together, the nine events of Gagne, Briggs, and Wager (1988) form the basis of the lesson plan. Each of the nine events is covered in a separate section of the plan, and the title of each gets distinctive graphical treatment. Recall that the events, which chapter 4 describes in detail, are as follows:

1. gaining attention
2. direction (stating objectives)
3. recall (recalling prerequisite information)
4. content (presentation of new material)
5. application feedback—level 1 (guided learning)
6. application feedback—level 2 (eliciting performance)
7. application feedback—level 3 (feedback)
8. evaluation (assessment)
9. closure (retention and transfer).

In the final plan, the name of each event appears in a box along with the suggested time needed for implementing that event. Designers may choose different labels for the sections, but, whatever name they use, they should let facilitators know how long each one should take to implement. For example:

```
Gaining Attention—5 minutes
```

Notations About Wording

The plan could provide information about what facilitators need to communicate but specify that they should put the information in their own words. The plan might say, for example:

"In your own words...
In the next hour that we have together, we will learn about working in teams."

The suggested language should be styled so that it is easy for the facilitator to spot it on the page.

Action Items

Action items may be set in boldface type to allow facilitators to see what they are expected to do next, as the following examples show:

▪ **Show slide #78.**
▪ **Start the video.**

In Conclusion

In this chapter, the process of designing an effective lesson plan was discussed. The nine events of instruction and suggestions for formatting were presented as considerations in lesson plan design. The CD includes a detailed exercise that covers the creation of a lesson plan and includes suggestions for success. As you answer the questions, you may consult the completed lesson plan for the poison prevention course, which is on the CD as well. The format for the poison prevention course begins with a checklist of activities that start 24 hours before the course and lead up to the beginning of the course. The plan goes on to detail the nine events of instruction in a section that contains the actual course. Designers who use a format with descriptive notes to facilitators make it much easier to obtain success with the course.

Putting What You Have Learned Into Action

Now, it's your turn to build a lesson plan. In exercises 9-1 and 9-2 on the CD, you have the option of using content for your own course, or you may use the subject matter from the poison prevention course. Either way, work through each exercise to build the lesson plan. If any of the elements presents a challenge for you, you may check the completed lesson plan on the CD.

Section 4 The Quality Rating Process and Tools

10 Quality Rating for Objectives: The QRO

Chapter Objectives

At the conclusion of this chapter, you should be able to

- describe the quality control process and identify tools for objectives, design plans, and lesson plans
- describe the format for the quality rating for objectives
- complete a QRO for a four-part objective.

Quality Control in ISD

As you advance your skills as an instructional designer, it will be important to establish a system of quality control that allows an unbiased and objective evaluation of ISD projects. The work you review may be your own, something you have been asked to review for someone else, or the work of your department or employees. Regardless of the source of the work, you need a benchmark for each of your design elements that allows you to gauge quality.

The quality rating evaluation instruments presented in this section of the book are just one example of the way you can accomplish this task. Whether you choose to use these as they are or modify them to fit your work environment and process, it is important that you elevate your professional skill standards as your experience allows. The very fact that you have a quality review process says much about your approach to ISD and your commitment to professional standards.

Quality Rating Matrices

There are three quality rating instruments making their debut in this book. All are intended to make the process of reviewing your ISD project more organized and standardized. The three matrices are

- quality rating for objectives
- quality rating for design plans
- quality rating for lesson plans.

Each of these quality rating tools is based on the standard instructional design formats appearing in this book. As you review the quality rating for objectives, you'll see that it is based on the A-B-C-D format for objectives. The quality rating for design plans format is based on the basic design elements most designers use. The quality rating for lesson plans is based on the nine-events format.

You will probably find yourself modifying these quality tools to fit your needs. These are meant to get you thinking and then moving toward establishing a quality control process for your work.

Quality Rating for Objectives

Writing objectives is both art and science. As such, it retains the best and worst qualities of subjective and objective thinking on the part of instructional designers. To make the process of reviewing the quality of formal ISD objectives more, well, objective, it helps to have a standard tool for evaluating them. The *quality rating for objectives* (QRO) is just such a tool.

The use of the QRO requires a standard from which to benchmark the quality of each individual objective, whether terminal or enabling. The standard described in this chapter has its genesis in the key elements of an objective as presented in this book. It can be modified for individual settings, but it gives you a basis for establishing your own standards either for an organization or as a personal standard for quality.

All the elements of an A-B-C-D objective (audience, behavior, condition, degree) are based on standards that conform to sound practice in ISD. Each of these elements is then assigned a numeric value; when summed, the values should total 100 percent for each objective.

Audience

Although the audience statement of an objective is simple in theory, writing a great audience statement is not always easy. The use of the wording *student, learner,* or *participant* is not always the best choice for your objective. Great ISD practice requires that you be much more specific and actually name the course or population as clearly as possible.

For the QRO, consider the three elements of the audience statement:

■ *Clarity:* Who is the intended audience? The term "learner" or another generic term is not sufficiently clear.

■ *Format:* How well is the audience statement written? Does it make sense?

■ *Perspective:* Is it written from the perspective of a single learner, rather than from that of a group, a facilitator, an organization, and so forth?

The matrix in table 10-1 can be used to rate the audience element. The maximum score for an audience statement is 20 percent of the 100 percent total for each objective.

Behavior

The behavior statement is the most important element in any objective and that importance is reflected in the QRO. The elements of importance to use in the QRO are

■ *Observable:* Is this a behavior that is tangible or is it ambiguous?

■ *Measurable:* Is it possible to measure learner mastery?

■ *Format:* How well is it written? Does the behavior statement make sense?

Table 10-2 is a matrix for rating the behavior element. The total for this element is 40 percent of the quality rating, a very significant part of the total.

Table 10-1. Rating the audience statement of an objective using QRO.

	Maximum Value (%)	Rating (%)
Clarity	10	
Format	5	
Perspective	5	

Table 10-2. Rating the behavior statement of an objective using QRO.

	Maximum Value (%)	Rating (%)
Observable	15	
Measurable	20	
Format	5	

Condition

When measuring condition elements it is important to make sure that each objective has a clear foundation of what will be provided within the learner-objective relationship. An objective lacking in conditions is many times unstable instructionally.

The QRO should address three areas of condition statements:

- ■ *Clarity:* Are all the conditions clearly defined in the objective?
- ■ *Comprehensiveness:* Are all the conditions mentioned?
- ■ *Format:* How well is the condition statement written? Does it make sense?

Table 10-3 depicts the QRO matrix for the condition statement. You can have a maximum of 20 percent for your condition element.

Degree

The value of a degree statement in an objective can never be understated; however, it is one of the most neglected elements in most of the objectives written. Consider these three very important elements of degree statements in the QRO:

- ■ *Clarity:* Is there any doubt about what is expected? Does the objective use any ambiguous language including "-ly" words such as "safely," "carefully," or "honestly."
- ■ *Measurable:* Is the degree statement in a format that is measurable?
- ■ *Format:* How well is it written? Does it make sense?

The QRO for the degree statement will look something like table 10-4. The degree element has a maximum total of 20 percent.

Format for a QRO

Figure 10-1 shows how a QRO might appear in practice.

Table 10-3. Rating the condition statement of an objective using QRO.

	Maximum Value (%)	Rating (%)
Clarity	10	
Comprehensiveness	5	
Format	5	

Table 10-4. Rating the degree statement of an objective using QRO.

	Maximum Value (%)	Rating (%)
Clarity	10	
Measurable	5	
Format	5	

Figure 10-1. Example of quality rating for objectives (QRO).

	Maximum Value (%)	Rating (%)
Audience (A)		
Clarity	10	
Format	5	
Perspective	5	
	Subtotal (20%)	
Behavior (B)		
Observable	15	
Measurable	20	
Format	5	
	Subtotal (40%)	
Condition (C)		
Clarity	10	
Comprehensiveness	5	
Format	5	
	Subtotal (20%)	
Degree (D)		
Clarity	10	
Measurable	5	
Format	5	
	Subtotal (20%)	
Total (A+B+C+D)	**100% Maximum**	

Variations

It is entirely possible that you might decide to add or subtract elements or to change the rating criteria or ratios on your version of the QRO. You should feel empowered to change anything to match your needs. You will probably want to keep as close to a 100-point scale as possible to make your results consistent and to use numerical values that have a common meaning, such as the 100-percent scale used here.

In Conclusion

The QRO is an advanced instructional design diagnostic and quality control tool for objectives. Designers should modify this tool to conform to their specific format for objectives.

Putting What You Have Learned Into Action

Exercise 10-1, included on the CD, allows you to practice the QRO on several objectives of you choice. You may use some of the objectives from chapter 3 as examples for this exercise if you don't have any objectives of your own to plug into the QRO.

11 Quality Rating for Design Plans: The QRDP

Chapter Objectives

At the conclusion of this chapter, you should be able to

- describe the format for the quality rating for design plans
- complete a QRDP for a design plan.

Quality Rating for Design Plans

The design plan in ISD is the standard document of the profession. Whether you use the format used in this book, or some variation, the standard elements of a design plan are the instructional design equivalent of the blueprint in architecture.

The *quality rating for design plans* (QRDP) provides a common format to review your design plans and make some very objective judgments relating to the quality of each design plan document. As with all quality rating strategies used here, the specifics of your design elements will only vary with the specifics of your approach and will not diminish the usefulness of this instructional design tool.

Recall that a design plan consists of eight elements:

- rationale
- target population
- course description
- objectives
- evaluation strategy

- participant prerequisites
- facilitator prerequisites
- deliverables.

Each element is reviewed and assigned a numerical rating; the total for each design plan should be 100 percent.

Rationale

In reviewing a rationale, you want to consider whether it has met the basic requirements of presenting your project in a way that allows the reader, usually a non-designer, to catch the important elements of your plan. Is your rationale truly a short, concise mission statement that delivers the message you want to convey?

The QRDP rates the following elements of a rationale:

- *Mission:* Is it clear why this course exists?
- *Detail:* Does the rationale provide the details of the course including audience and sponsors?
- *Format:* Is it well written and as brief as possible? Does it make sense?

Table 11-1 is a matrix to help you rate the rationale element. With a total value of 13 percent, the rationale is an important foundation for your design plan and is weighted to reflect that importance.

Target Population

Defining a population within your design plan is a key element when starting your design. Most of your design decisions, including media, methods, and objectives will flow from this element of your design. Several important elements of your target population are reviewed in the QRDP:

- *Clarity:* Is it clear whom the population includes?
- *Detail:* How much do you actually know about the population? Is this enough?

Table 11-1. Rating the rationale element of a design plan using QRDP.

	Maximum Value (%)	Rating (%)
Mission	5	
Detail	5	
Format	3	

■ *Challenges:* Does this element of the design plan identify specifics—both positive and negative—about this population?

Table 11-2 provides a strategy for rating the target population element. Your maximum for the population element is 12 percent of the rating.

Course Description

Your course description is the logistics and methods element of your design plan. Make sure that all the detail you need for your project is here somewhere. As a minimum have at least these elements in your ratings:

■ *Course length:* Is it clear how this course is timed (how long, when, and so forth)?

■ *Instructional method:* How is this course implemented?

■ *Materials:* What does the facilitator need in terms of handouts, texts, video, audiovisual equipment, and so forth?

The ratings for the description element within the design plan are shown in table 11-3. The course description represents a maximum of 15 percent of your total.

Table 11-2. Rating the target population element of a design plan using QRDP.

	Maximum Value (%)	Rating (%)
Clarity	5	
Detail	5	
Challenges	2	

Table 11-3. Rating the course description element of a design plan using QRDP.

	Maximum Value (%)	Rating (%)
Course Length	5	
Instructional Methods	5	
Materials	5	

Objectives

Because objectives are the heart of your design plan, you want to make sure they are up to your quality standards. At this point in the quality rating process, you can either use the existing QRO matrix or you can just use the QRDP for more operational elements of the objectives in your plan. For this example we are going to use the latter approach.

- *Number:* Have you included all of the objectives that are needed for this content?
- *Format:* Are the objectives in the A-B-C-D format?
- *Detail:* Do you have both terminal and enabling objectives?

Table 11-4 shows the quality rating system for objectives. Your objectives have a maximum rating of 12 percent of the total.

Evaluation Strategy

This quality element actually involves all of the other elements in your design plan because you want to make sure that you have evaluated both the project and process involved in finalizing your design plan. Possible elements for this matrix include:

- *Detail:* Have you listed and explained your choices for evaluation (type, forms, and so forth)?
- *Process:* How will you implement your evaluation?
- *Thoroughness:* Have you been thorough in your evaluation process? Is it real?

The quality rating for evaluation in your design plan is shown in table 11-5. Evaluations are a maximum of 15 percent of your total rating.

Table 11-4. Rating the objectives of a design plan using QRDP.

	Maximum Value (%)	Rating (%)
Number	5	
Format	5	
Detail	2	

Table 11-5. Rating the evaluation strategy of a design plan using QRDP.

	Maximum Value (%)	Rating (%)
Detail	5	
Process	5	
Thoroughness	5	

Participant Prerequisites

Prerequisites are important to your design plan so make sure you have covered all the bases with your plan. Evaluate your participant prerequisites according to these criteria:

- ▪ *Clarity:* Is it clear which prerequisites each participant is required to meet?
- ▪ *Ranging:* Have you listed the highest and lowest recommended prerequisites?

Table 11-6 is a matrix you can use to rate your participant prerequisites in the design plan. Eight percent of the total score for the design plan represents the participant prerequisites.

Table 11-6. Rating the participant prerequisites of a design plan using QRDP.

	Maximum Value (%)	Rating (%)
Clarity	5	
Ranging	3	

Facilitator Prerequisites

Setting the standards for those that facilitate your course is an important aspect of instructional design. At a minimum, you should list the qualifications you expect from a facilitator. Be sure not to use vague wording or ambiguous standards. For example

- ▪ *Minimum standards:* Have you listed your expectations?
- ▪ *Clarity:* Are your standards clear and unambiguous?

Table 11-7 shows a method for rating your facilitator prerequisites in the design plan. Facilitator prerequisites comprise a maximum of 10 percent of your total.

Table 11-7. Rating the facilitator prerequisites of a design plan using QRDP.

	Maximum Value (%)	Rating (%)
Minimum Standards	5	
Clarity	5	

Deliverables

Knowing what is required for a project is a great communication tool for designers in working with both a design team and clients. Make sure you have considered the following:

- *Thoroughness:* Have you included everything?
- *Clarity:* Is it clear what each deliverable really is?
- *Responsibility:* Is it clear who is responsible for each deliverable?

Table 11-8 presents a matrix for evaluating the deliverables portion of your design plan. The importance of deliverables is reflected in the total score achieved toward the maximum of 15 percent of your total rating.

Table 11-8. Rating the deliverables element of a design plan using QRDP.

	Maximum Value (%)	Rating (%)
Thoroughness	5	
Clarity	5	
Responsibility	5	

Format for a QRDP

Figure 11-1 shows how a QRDP appears in practice.

In Conclusion

This chapter describes the QRDP and provides instructional designers a format for evaluating a design plan. Designers should feel comfortable modifying this format to fit variations in design plan formats, remembering to change the values to fit a 100-point scale.

Figure 11-1. Example of quality rating for design plans (QRDP).

	Maximum Value (%)	Rating (%)
Rationale		
Mission	5	
Detail	5	
Format	3	
	Subtotal (13%)	
Target Population		
Clarity	5	
Detail	5	
Challenges	2	
	Subtotal (12%)	
Course Description		
Course Length	5	
Instructional Methods	5	
Materials	5	
	Subtotal (15%)	
Objectives		
Number	5	
Format	5	
Detail	2	
	Subtotal (12%)	
Evaluation Strategy		
Detail	5	
Process	5	
Thoroughness	5	
	Subtotal (15%)	

(continued on next page)

Figure 11-1. Example of quality rating for design plans (QRDP) (continued).

	Maximum Value (%)	Rating (%)
Participant Prerequisites		
Clarity	5	
Ranging	3	
	Subtotal (8%)	
Facilitator Prerequisites		
Minimum Standards	5	
Clarity	5	
	Subtotal (10%)	
Deliverables		
Thoroughness	5	
Clarity	5	
Responsibility	5	
	Subtotal (15%)	
Total	**100% Maximum**	

Putting What You Have Learned Into Action

Using the supplied QRDP form, exercise 11-1 on the CD, apply the QRDP to a design plan of your choice. You can always use the poison prevention design plan as your example for review. As with all of the quality rating instruments, feel free to modify the sections to fit your design plan format if it is different from the format used in the book.

12 Quality Rating for Lesson Plans: The QRLP

Chapter Objectives

At the conclusion of this chapter, you should be able to

- describe the format for the quality rating for lesson plans
- complete a QRLP for a standard nine-element lesson plan.

Quality Rating for Lesson Plans

The lesson plan in ISD is a standard document of learning professionals spanning the gamut from kindergarten teachers to corporate coaches. Whether you use the exact format used in this book or some variation, the standard nine elements of a lesson plan are included in the *quality rating for lesson plans* (QRLP). Each of the first eight elements also includes a rating for transition. This rating measures how well one element flows into the following element. Stated otherwise, do all the elements fit together to create a comprehensive whole? This is important because a lesson plan should appear seamless to the learner.

Each of the nine elements of a lesson plan are reviewed and assigned a numeric rating; totaling the individual ratings should yield a maximum of 100 percent for each lesson plan.

Gaining Attention

In this first element, make sure you have started the process of focusing a learner on the task at hand. Is it short but powerful, and does it relate to the formal objectives in your design plan? Consider these criteria as you evaluate this element:

- *Gains attention:* How well does it begin focusing a learner's attention on the content?
- *Brevity:* Does it last less than five minutes?
- *Relates to content:* Is there a direct correlation?
- *Transition:* How well does this element flow to the next?

Table 12-1 shows criteria for evaluating the strength of your lesson plan in terms of gaining the attention of participants. Gaining attention accounts for 12 percent of your total in the QRLP.

Direction

This section of your lesson plan is where you present your objectives and you want to be both clear and complete in the way you do this aspect of your lesson plan.

- *Objectives present:* Are the program objectives clearly identified?
- *Clarity:* Is it clear what you are asking learners to do?
- *Transition:* How well does this element flow to the next?

Evaluate the direction element of your lesson plan using the criteria laid out in table 12-2. Direction accounts for 12 percent of your QRLP.

Recall

This key lesson plan element serves as a safety net for learners, so make sure that key prerequisites are reviewed and any deficits in knowledge or performance are addressed before you start with the new content. Ask yourself these questions:

Table 12-1. Rating the gaining attention element of a lesson plan using QRLP.

	Maximum Value (%)	Rating (%)
Gains Attention	5	
Brevity	2	
Relates to Content	3	
Transition	2	

Table 12-2. Rating the direction element of a lesson plan using QRLP.

	Maximum Value (%)	Rating (%)
Objectives Present	5	
Clarity	5	
Transition	2	

■ *Key prerequisite content covered:* Have you covered all of the necessary prerequisites?

■ *Strategies for over- and underqualified learners:* Have you allowed for both over- and underqualified learners?

■ *Transition:* How well does this element flow to the next?

Recall constitutes 9 percent of your QRLP total. You can use the matrix in table 12-3 for evaluating the recall element.

Content

This is the heart of your lesson plan. Be sure to present the content in an ordered and dynamic format; make it real for your learners.

■ *Lively:* Is it more than just boring regurgitation of content?

■ *Clarity:* Is the content detailed and clear in the way it is presented?

■ *Transition:* How well does this element lead to the next?

Content accounts for 11 percent of your QRLP total. Use the scoring system outlined in table 12-4 for evaluating this element.

Table 12-3. Rating the recall element of a lesson plan using QRLP.

	Maximum Value (%)	Rating (%)
Key Prerequisite Content Covered	5	
Strategies for Over- and Underqualified Learners	2	
Transition	2	

Table 12-4. Rating the content element of a lesson plan using QRLP.

	Maximum Value (%)	Rating (%)
Lively	5	
Clarity	4	
Transition	2	

Application Feedback—Level 1

Now you are ready to reinforce your content and at this first level you need to have your facilitation at an equal keel with your learners—a joint engagement of content-related interaction with focused and precise feedback. Consider the following:

- *50:50 facilitator-learner ratio:* Is this an even engagement?
- *Application feedback opportunity:* Is there feedback provided?
- *Clarity:* Is the feedback clear from a learner's perspective?
- *Transition:* How well does this element flow to the next?

Table 12-5 presents a method for evaluating application feedback—level 1, which accounts for 13 percent of your QRLP total.

Application Feedback—Level 2

At this point you want to start handing off the ownership of the content to the learner. Small-group work is an example of an implementation modality.

- *30:70 facilitator-learner ratio:* Are you handing off ownership to the learner at this point in the lesson plan?

Table 12-5. Rating the application feedback—level 1 element of a lesson plan using QRLP.

	Maximum Value (%)	Rating (%)
50:50 Facilitator-Learner Ratio	4	
Application Feedback—Level 1 Opportunity	4	
Clarity	2	
Transition	3	

■ *Application feedback—level 2 opportunity:* Is there feedback provided?

■ *Clarity:* Is it clear?

■ *Transition:* How well does this element flow to the next?

Application feedback—level 2 accounts for 13 percent of your QRLP total. Break down the scoring of this element as shown in table 12-6.

Application Feedback—Level 3

Now is the time to provide the learners with almost all of the ownership of the content. Think of this as the pre-evaluation phase of your lesson plan.

■ *10:90 facilitator-learner ratio:* Are learners really in control of the content?

■ *Application feedback—level 3 opportunity:* Is there feedback provided?

■ *Clarity:* Is the feedback clear from the learner's perspective?

■ *Transition:* How well does this element flow to the next?

Application feedback—level 3 accounts for 13 percent of your QRLP total, as shown in table 12-7.

Evaluation

Now that learners have had three opportunities to practice the objectives, they are ready for the formal evaluation—if it exists. If not, have you designed a process for facilitators to double-check previous informal evaluations from application feedback elements at levels 1, 2, and 3?

■ *Evaluation present:* Does an evaluation actually take place in this element?

■ *Clarity:* Is the evaluation component clear?

■ *Transition:* How well does this element flow to the next?

Table 12-6. Rating the application feedback—level 2 element of a lesson plan using QRLP.

	Maximum Value (%)	Rating (%)
30:70 Facilitator-Learner Ratio	4	
Application Feedback—Level 2 Opportunity	4	
Clarity	2	
Transition	3	

Table 12-7. Rating the application feedback—level 3 element of a lesson plan using QRLP.

	Maximum Value (%)	Rating (%)
10:90 Facilitator-Learner Ratio	4	
Application Feedback— Level 3 Opportunity	4	
Clarity	2	
Transition	3	

Evaluation accounts for 9 percent of your QRLP total. See table 12-8 for a systematic way of assessing the evaluation element of your lesson plan.

Closure

Closure—the final element of your lesson plan—is your last chance to perform a quality check. Make sure you also recap the lesson and apply any opportunities to generalize and synthesize the content from the lesson.

- *Recap of content:* Have you reviewed the objectives?
- *Generalization:* Have you generalized the content?
- *Synthesis:* Have you synthesized the content?

Table 12-9 is a systematic means of evaluating your closure element. Closure accounts for 8 percent of your QRLP total.

Format for a QRLP

Figure 12-1 brings together the whole QRLP instrument; you could use this or a similar model for evaluating your own lesson plans.

Table 12-8. Rating the evaluation element of a lesson plan using QRLP.

	Maximum Value (%)	Rating (%)
Evaluation Present	5	
Clarity	2	
Transition	2	

In Conclusion

This chapter describes the QRLP and provides instructional designers an objective format for evaluating a lesson plan. Designers should feel comfortable modifying this format to fit variations in lesson plan formats, remembering to change the values to fit a 100-point scale.

Table 12-9. Rating the closure element of a lesson plan using QRLP.

	Maximum Value (%)	Rating (%)
Recap of Content	4	
Generalization	2	
Synthesis	2	

Figure 12-1. Example of quality rating for lesson plans (QRLP).

	Maximum Value (%)	Rating (%)
Gaining Attention		
Gains Attention	5	
Brevity	2	
Relates to Content	3	
Transition	2	
	Subtotal (12%)	
Direction		
Objectives Present	5	
Clarity	5	
Transition	2	
	Subtotal (12%)	

(continued on next page)

Figure 12-1. Example of quality rating for lesson plans (QRLP) (continued).

	Maximum Value (%)	Rating (%)
Recall		
Key Prerequisite Content Covered	5	
Strategies for Over- and Underqualified Learners	2	
Transition	2	
	Subtotal (9%)	
Content		
Lively	5	
Clarity	4	
Transition	2	
	Subtotal (11%)	
Application Feedback— Level 1		
50:50 Facilitator-Learner Ratio	4	
Application Feedback— Level 2 Opportunity	4	
Clarity	2	
Transition	3	
	Subtotal (13%)	
Application Feedback— Level 2		
30:70 Facilitator-Learner Ratio	4	
Application Feedback— Level 2 Opportunity	4	
Clarity	2	
Transition	3	
	Subtotal (13%)	

	Maximum Value (%)	Rating (%)
Application Feedback— Level 3		
10:90 Facilitator-Learner Ratio	4	
Application Feedback— Level 3 Opportunity	4	
Clarity	2	
Transition	3	
	Subtotal (13%)	
Evaluation		
Evaluation Present	5	
Clarity	2	
Transition	2	
	Subtotal (9%)	
Closure		
Recap of Content	4	
Generalization	2	
Synthesis	2	
	Subtotal (8%)	
Total	**100% Maximum**	

Putting What You Have Learned Into Action

Using the supplied QRLP form, exercise 12-1 on the CD, apply the QRLP to a lesson plan of your choice. You can always use the poison prevention lesson plan as your example for review. As with all of the quality rating instruments, feel free to modify the sections to fit your lesson plan format if it is different from the nine events format used in the book.

13 The Criticality Matrix System for Content Selection

At the conclusion of this chapter, you should be able to

- define the need for a matrix system for content selection
- list the four levels of objective criticality
- list the five criticality matrices
- define the key elements of each matrix level
- provide at least one example for each of the five matrices.

Making Tough Content Decisions

It is the rare course that has just the right amount of content for time allocated for implementation. It always seems as though you either have too little time or too much content. Although some decisions about what goes and what stays are easily made, most are not. If the process is further complicated by such variables as required content or if you have to navigate a minefield of polarizing opinions held by various decision makers, then you have a recipe for chaos. In such situations, ISD can come to the rescue with a logical way to work through content systematically by providing a way to rate each objective or skill using a system that allows content to make the tough decisions for you, based on the relationship of the content to the other design elements.

The logic of this approach lies in the way you rate each skill or objective based on several critical values related to the course. Specifically, they are

- criticality of the content
- frequency of application by a learner
- relationship between criticality and frequency of application.

To apply ISD in this process, you need to turn to a system of *criticality matrices* that provides conclusive data, which can then be used in a way that works within your design environment. It almost makes decisions for you if you let it, or you can simply take the data and use it within a design group for discussion.

Five matrices together provide *criticality data:*

- level 1—criticality
- level 2—frequency of application
- level 3—criticality and frequency of application
- level 4—ranking
- level 5—disposition.

Let's look and see how each matrix works alone and in concert with others to form the criticality system.

Level 1—Criticality

Table 13-1 is a level 1 criticality matrix for rating each objective or content element based on its level of criticality within the course in one of the following ranges:

- critical
- essential
- prerequisite
- ineffectual.

Although you undoubtedly will evolve your own definition of each of these classifications, it might help to look at the range of each of these classifications.

Table 13-1. Level 1 criticality matrix.

Rating	Objective One	Objective Two	Objective Three
Critical Objective			
Essential Objective			
Prerequisite Objective			
Ineffectual Objective			

Critical. Critical objectives are those that cannot under any circumstance be omitted from your course. Among them are

- *mandated critical:* objectives involving required legal or technical content
- *performance critical:* objectives that because of the severity of the consequences of omission or poor performance must be included
- *organizational critical:* required for reasons other than mandate or performance, for example, internal political issues, policy, or practice.

Essential. Essential objectives are those objectives that are not critical but are required for a thorough course in the content area. Examples are

- *skill steps:* detailed content or procedures on a particular skill or concept
- *objective domain specific:* objectives that match a required domain requirement, for example, teaching learners specifics of a skill rather than just providing an overview.

Prerequisite. Prerequisite objectives cover content that is sometimes marginal in terms of necessity for implementation but is useful as background information or for ensuring learning conformance with prerequisites. Examples include the following:

- *relevant policy, practice, or organizational procedures:* setting the background
- *skills review:* equations, safety rules
- *adjunct information:* background readings, history, or added detail on a topic.

Ineffectual. Ineffectual objectives are just about every other objective you may have and that are not always easy to eliminate. This classification can cause distress in group or team settings where decisions need to be made to shorten a course and issues other than content are involved. For example

- *loyalty content:* the video of the organization's president adds nothing to the course
- *political content:* objectives that are clearly meant to aid organizational presence but offer little or no tangible content.

Level 2—Frequency of Application

In this matrix, shown in table 13-2, you measure the relative value of specific objectives based on the application of the content by a learner. This value is averaged over a population with the acceptance of the fact that each individual learner will apply this content in somewhat different ways.

Table 13-2. Level 2 criticality matrix—frequency of application.

Application	Objective One	Objective Two	Objective Three
Daily			
Weekly			
Monthly			
Quarterly			
Yearly			
Never			

Level 3—Criticality and Frequency of Application

It is now time to combine the criticality and frequency of application data into one matrix (table 13-3), providing you with another dimension for comparison of objectives. It is important to add this additional data matrix because critical objectives that are used most often by learners will trend toward the high range on this scale. Similarly, less important objectives that are seldom if ever used by learners trend toward the bottom of the scale.

Table 13-3. Level 3 criticality matrix—criticality and frequency of application.

Objective One	Critical (3)	Essential (2)	Prerequisite (1)	Ineffectual (0)
Daily (5)				
Weekly (4)				
Monthly (3)				
Quarterly (2)				
Yearly (1)				
Never (0)				

Level 4—Ranking

Now, using a matrix similar to that shown in table 13-4, you need to rank all of your objectives against one another by using the data from the previous matrix (table 13-3). This process provides you with clear and concise placement for each objective and makes the process of choosing objectives much easier.

Level 5—Disposition

Now is the time to make the final decisions about your objectives and to chart those decisions in this matrix. This matrix, based on the format of table 13-5, will probably be the final worksheet you'll need for preparing your design plan.

Table 13-4. Level 4 criticality matrix—ranking.

Ranking	8	7	6	5	4	3	2	1	0
Objective One									
Objective Two									
Objective Three									

Table 13-5. Level 5 criticality matrix—disposition.

Disposition	Objective One	Objective Two	Objective Three
Mandatory			
Recommended			
Optional			
Work/Job Aid			
Prerequisite			
Precourse Reading			
Postcourse Reading			
Unnecessary			

Working Through an Example

Now you'll have the chance to work through the operation of the criticality matrix system using a real-world example. Let's say that you are going to make critical content decisions for a course entitled Safety in the Workplace for first-year apprentices in the building trades.

You have the following terminal objectives to make determinations concerning final disposition in a four-hour course. For this exercise, draft objective wording will be used because you are still in the early stages of the design process and would not yet have formalized the objectives into four parts (A-B-C-D).

- Objective One: should be able to state OSHA regulation(s) concerning hard hat use.
- Objective Two: should be able to demonstrate recommended hard hat use.
- Objective Three: should be able to list union/company policy on hard hat use.
- Objective Four: should be able to cite possible types of head injury resulting from failing to use a hard hat.
- Objective Five: should be able to list sources for purchasing hard hats.

Now we will work through the level 1 matrix using our five objectives. Table 13-6 represents a possible scenario for these objectives.

Although you might not agree with my rating for each of these objectives, it is clear that there is a pattern of criticality based on these choices. Objective two is considered critical, objective four is essential, and the remaining objectives (one, three, and five) are considered prerequisite. What this tells us as instructional designers is that we have a clear road map to use for gauging inclusion of objectives. If you have time for implementing all five objectives, you are fine. If there's

Table 13-6. Level 1 criticality matrix (Safety in the Workplace course).

Rating	Objective One	Objective Two	Objective Three	Objective Four	Objective Five
Critical		X			
Essential				X	
Prerequisite	X		X		X
Ineffectual					

time for implementing two objectives, you also have a clear guide to follow—objectives two and four will be included, and the remaining objectives would be prerequisites or pre- or postcourse reading assignments.

The level 2 matrix allows you to dig deeper into objectives when the issues are not so clear-cut as those in the first example. Assume that there is some disagreement about the outcome of the first matrix and you need to dig deeper to see which objectives should be included. Now, you will include the frequency of application data for review.

Table 13-7 depicts how we might rate these objectives in terms of the frequency of application.

Now you can see a definite pattern starting to appear for our five objectives. The second objective is also something that a learner will probably use every working day on the job. The other four objectives will probably find less frequent use with one actually having only yearly value in terms of learner implementation. Again, you can argue with my rating, but those decisions can be made as a group and ironed out in the course of the conversation. We have now further refined our content criticality to the point where a single objective, objective two, is by far the most important for this course.

Now, let's make your head swim! We are going to further define each of our objectives using the level 3 matrix, which adds each objective's rating (from the level 1 matrix) and application (from the level 2 matrix), arriving at a final, multi-dimensional criticality.

Table 13-8 shows the matrix completed for objective one, which we rated as prerequisite in terms of criticality and monthly in terms of frequency.

Table 13-7. Level 2 criticality matrix—frequency of application (Safety in the Workplace course).

Application	Objective One	Objective Two	Objective Three	Objective Four	Objective Five
Daily		X			
Weekly					
Monthly	X		X		
Quarterly				X	
Yearly					X
Never					

Table 13-8. Level 3 criticality matrix—rating + frequency of application (Safety in the Workplace course, objective one).

Objective One	Critical (3)	Essential (2)	Prerequisite (1)	Ineffectual (0)
Daily (5)				
Weekly (4)				
Monthly (3)			4	
Quarterly (2)				
Yearly (1)				
Never (0)				

As you can see we added the two values from the first two matrices and came up with a rating of 4 for this objective. Tables 13-9 through 13-12 show the level 3 criticality matrices for the remaining four objectives.

We now need to rank our five objectives based on the last matrix results (table 13-13).

Table 13-9. Level 3 criticality matrix—rating + frequency of application (Safety in the Workplace course, objective two).

Objective Two	Critical (3)	Essential (2)	Prerequisite (1)	Ineffectual (0)
Daily (5)	8			
Weekly (4)				
Monthly (3)				
Quarterly (2)				
Yearly (1)				
Never (0)				

Table 13-10. Level 3 criticality matrix—rating + frequency of application (Safety in the Workplace course, objective three).

Objective Three	Critical (3)	Essential (2)	Prerequisite (1)	Ineffectual (0)
Daily (5)				
Weekly (4)				
Monthly (3)			4	
Quarterly (2)				
Yearly (1)				
Never (0)				

Table 13-11. Level 3 criticality matrix—rating + frequency of application (Safety in the Workplace course, objective four).

Objective Four	Critical (3)	Essential (2)	Prerequisite (1)	Ineffectual (0)
Daily (5)				
Weekly (4)				
Monthly (3)				
Quarterly (2)		4		
Yearly (1)				
Never (0)				

Table 13-12. Level 3 criticality matrix—rating + frequency of application (Safety in the Workplace course, objective five).

Objective Five	Critical (3)	Essential (2)	Prerequisite (1)	Ineffectual (0)
Daily (5)				
Weekly (4)				
Monthly (3)				
Quarterly (2)				
Yearly (1)			2	
Never (0)				

Table 13-13. Level 4 criticality matrix—ranking (Safety in the Workplace course).

Ranking	8	7	6	5	4	3	2	1	0
Objective 1					X				
Objective 2	X								
Objective 3					X				
Objective 4					X				
Objective 5							X		

This tells us that objective two has the highest ranking (8), with objectives one, three, and four tied for the next highest ranking (4). Objective five is a distant last with a 2 ranking.

Table 13-14 shows an alternative priority ranking matrix with the objectives appearing in order of decreasing priority.

Our final matrix (table 13-15) provides the final disposition for each objective.

Table 13-14. Level 4 criticality matrix—ranking (Safety in the Workplace course, alternative ranking).

Ranking	8	7	6	5	4	3	2	1	0
Objective 2	X								
Objective 1					X				
Objective 3					X				
Objective 4					X				
Objective 5							X		

Table 13-15. Level 5 criticality matrix—disposition (Safety in the Workplace course).

Disposition	Objective 1	Objective 2	Objective 3	Objective 4	Objective 5
Mandatory		X			
Recommended	X		X	X	
Optional					
Work/Job Aid					X
Prerequisite					
Precourse Reading					
Postcourse Reading					
Unnecessary					

In Conclusion

At this point, you have worked through five levels of criticality and resolved the disposition of each objective in this limited sample from a Safety in the Workplace course.

Depending on your situation, it may not be necessary to use each of these steps to make decisions. However, you now have the mechanism available to you to work with other designers, SMEs, and clients on these issues. This process works equally well if you are working solo but need to make critical decisions about objectives.

Putting What You Have Learned Into Action

Now it's time to take the concepts involved in criticality and start working through an example that contains your content so that you can get a feel for how the process works. Use exercises 13-1 to 13-5 on the companion CD to do this.

14 Designing for Academic Credit

Chapter Objectives

At the conclusion of this chapter, you should be able to

- describe at least two general requirements for credit consideration when designing a course
- implement a credit review for a design plan
- modify a design plan to improve the likelihood of obtaining credit for a course.

One critical value-added element of instructional design, often treated tangentially outside of academic institutions, is to engage a design philosophy that ensures that each course has the potential to provide participants with academic credit. A *credit-for-courses design* philosophy includes a system for making sure that academic course requirements are considered at each step in the design process. In most cases, this is not a difficult task because well-designed courses have many of these elements already; it is often just a matter of packing the data in such a way that each course has the potential to be reviewed for credit worthiness by a credit-granting college or university or by the American Council on Education (ACE, http://www.acenet.edu/).

Credit: What It Takes

To be clear, courses accepted for college credit include more than just a great set of objectives. These courses must meet a system of requirements that involves contact hours, requirements for instructors, evaluation, record keeping, content rigor, and numerous other elements that must be met to ensure creditworthiness for a course or program. This is where an instructional designer can easily take the basic ISD deliverables of a design plan and lesson plan and expand them to create the necessary framework for academic review.

This goes well beyond the concept of providing credit in the form of *continuing education units* (CEU), sometimes called *professional development units* (PDU), which are often a recognition of attendance, not participation or evaluation. These are usually offered, for a fee, at a ratio of one CEU for each 10 hours of attendance. CEUs are often used in professional training settings where college credit is not an issue for attendees, but in-service training is often required for licensure, for example, for medical doctors, lawyers, and accountants. Their usefulness for credit-seeking learners is often limited at best because CEUs are not generally accepted by academic programs as credit toward a degree. As with anything academic, there are exceptions to this general rule. Investigate thoroughly, and find out what works best for you in any given circumstance.

Designing for credit begins with the recognition that most occupational and learning activities that adults engage in are worthy of consideration for college credit. There are countless examples of where life-educated individuals demonstrate equal or greater skills in a specific area than a college-educated individual with no life experience in the same content area.

Many colleges and universities offer credit for life experience, and these credits are often requested through the development of a portfolio that consists of a series of credit requests based on the life experience of the learner. Experiential credits are always capped at a set number by the college or university accepting them. These policies are further defined by academic accrediting bodies and state accrediting organizations.

Although experiential learning credits are an important aspect of earning college credits for millions of adults, there is something more that designers can do to help turn learning by adults into credits recognized by many colleges and universities. Going the extra step of having a course or series of courses reviewed and awarded credit allows learners the opportunity to bring credit to an academic institution that they are attending or request credit through the life experience process.

Exploring Credit Options

Academic and experiential credit opportunities work in partnership to offer important options for learners. Although the details of how this works in each college or university are generally similar, it is beyond the scope of this book to detail how the credits are accepted (or not) by individual schools, programs, or content majors. Moreover, the cost for moving these credits to a transcript varies widely from one school to another. What is important is that the design process allows the option for courses to be reviewed for credit if that is something that is important to the population the courses will serve.

ACE has a program called the College Credit Recommendation Service. This program allows ACE to review courses and then potentially offer credit recommendations for these courses. ACE has reviewed and made credit recommendations regarding thousands of courses. It is then up to an individual academic institution to review and consider accepting these credits for individual students. You should contact ACE directly for specific details of the costs, requirements, and process. An excellent book entitled *Pocket Guide to College Credits and Degrees: Valuable Information for Adult Learners* (Johnson, Robinson, & Welch, 2004), written primarily for adult learners, helps explain some of the issues related to earning lifelong learning credits, accreditation, and other issues.

This process can also sometimes be accomplished by working directly with a college or university in a partnership that allows courses to be included as part of a specific program within a school. In this case, the course or courses will have to comply with the requirements of the school and may have to be reviewed by a faculty committee and approved by one or more levels of academic accrediting requirements at the local, regional, or national level.

Two important elements that most potential accrediting bodies require in a course or program are

■ *Stability of implementation and content:* In other words, is the same course that is approved going to be offered each time at every location by each facilitator? A credit course needs to have a minimum number of contact hours, evaluation, and content at each implementation. If you have multiple field locations, all must offer the course exactly as approved.

■ *Record keeping:* How will attendance, evaluation, and facilitator data be gathered and kept?

ISD and having a professional design and lesson plan offer you incredible support in this endeavor. Because your system contains these elements, it is much easier to design for credit right from the start, and you can offer accrediting organizations very persuasive evidence that you will offer a stable and replicable course or program across a variety of facilitators and sites.

One great advantage of using ISD as your design process is that many of the elements of ISD that you use naturally lend themselves to credit standards. The most obvious element of ISD that works well with this process is the body of objectives.

Well-written terminal and enabling objectives will go a long way toward providing a credit foundation, and little consideration will be given for credit to courses that do not have a solid set of objectives.

No matter how you intend to move your courses into a credit environment, designing a course around a credit framework gets you a step closer to having credit awarded for learners that successfully complete a course you design. Even if college credit opportunities are not necessarily the focus of your sponsor or population, the structure of your course will be sound if you are designing with creditworthiness in mind.

Partnerships

Many colleges and universities, especially community colleges, are interested in partnerships with unions, businesses, and other organizations that offer them an opportunity to expand their student base. A key ingredient in these partnerships is the courses offered to students by the nonacademic partner. An excellent example of this relationship is apprenticeship programs offered by building trades unions that are linked to degree programs at an academic partner. Many apprentices now have the opportunity to turn their training into college credit through ACE credits and partnership programs. There is no reason that this same process can't work for almost every training course.

Designing for Credit

Some general rules apply to courses that are designed to be creditworthy. Although there are many variations on this theme, always keep these issues foremost in your design approach:

- *College-level content:* Make sure that your content is at least at a post-secondary educational level or that a similar course is offered somewhere in an accredited college or university. The easiest way to do this is to review course descriptions from various colleges or universities in the content area you are covering in your course.
- *Solid objectives using at a minimum the A-B-C-D structure:* Excellent objectives always reflect professional course design standards and are recognized as a sign of sound design practice in an instructional designer.
- *Tangible evaluation tasks that are implemented at the level of the individual student:* This must be more than just a student listening at a conference. You must have real evaluation that links directly to objectives. This is the performance agreement principle in practice. See chapter 3 for more information concerning performance agreement.

- *Contact hour ratios of at least 15:1 (hours:credits):* This is the standard in many, but not all, situations relating to student seat-time. Ratios for field-work are usually much higher, sometimes 1,500:1 or more. If you are working with modules that are less than 15 hours in length, consider grouping courses into a program that meets the requirement in terms of minimum contact hours. For example, two eight-hour courses might be bundled as a 16-hour program for one credit.

- *Materials and texts that are college level in content:* This is always a bit subjective, but make sure that any materials and texts meet an acceptable level of sophistication relative to the content.

- *Instructor prerequisites:* Academic institutions usually require that the instructor of record have a degree at least one level above the level being taught (bachelor's for an associate's, master's for bachelor's, for example). There are numerous variations on this requirement in different situations, but it is worth keeping in mind as you design your course.

- *Record keeping:* Records must reflect each individual student's attendance, evaluation, and final disposition within the course. These records usually are shared with the academic institution for eventual placement on a student transcript.

- *Student participation and competence:* To receive academic credit, courses must have standards for acceptable student participation. This is sometimes a letter grading system or some variation of the pass/no credit grading option. Make sure the student is informed of the grade received.

The design plan is where most of the information relating to creditworthiness appears. The design plan is a reflection of the system that is developed for a course. The elements in the design plan provide the perfect platform for this information and are already uniquely positioned to accept the additional detail for this process. A well-written design plan is vital to this process. Let's look at each element of the design plan as it relates to the design-for-credit philosophy.

Rationale

Because this is the mission statement for your course, there are several elements of your rationale that will support your credit request:

- *Organizational purpose:* It is vital that you provide detailed information concerning the organization sponsoring the course, specifically relating to the mission of the organization that includes providing education and training to adults.

- *Organizational endorsement:* It must be clear that the organization is sponsoring this course. Identical courses offered by different sponsors are not always identical in the eyes of an accrediting body.
- *Organizational structure:* It must be clear, at a minimum, that the sponsoring group has the capacity for record keeping and other necessary administrative functions.
- *Education goal:* The course should contain material at a postsecondary level.

Target Population

Defining your population is critical to seeking credit. As you identify the target population, keep in mind the following:

- *Age of the target population:* Generally, participants must be at least 18 years old.
- *Application:* You need to make the case that participants will be able to use the course for professional or academic advancement, usually a degree, certificate, or licensure.

Course Description

The detail contained in the course description provides several key elements of information for the process of seeking credits for the course:

- *Implementation time:* The number of contact hours for a course is critical to determining creditworthiness and value. Remember that a ratio of 15:1 (contact hours to credit) is often used as a guideline.
- *Instructional methods:* Be sure to list the different types of methods you will use in your course including instructor-led learning, case studies, role plays, online instruction, and so forth.
- *Course administration:* Delineate how the course will be implemented in operational terms including the record keeping elements of attendance and evaluation.
- *Materials:* List all materials including handouts, texts, and formal evaluation instruments.

Objectives

Objectives are the heart of your design plan. Here are several things to remember:

- *Detail:* Make sure your objectives are written in the most detailed way possible.
- *Format:* Do not stray from the A-B-C-D format because it is a common method of writing objectives in professional and academic environments.

- *Domain:* Be sure to include the primary and any secondary objective domains.
- *Clarity:* They must by measurable and observable, without exception.

Evaluation Strategy

Credit requires evaluation, and this element of your design plan allows you to show-case your evaluation strategy for a course. Although this is a common element of ISD, here are several things to keep in mind while working on evaluation in your plan:

- *Technique:* Make it painfully obvious how you are going to evaluate learners—detail, detail, and more detail.
- *Performance agreement:* Every objective must be evaluated and in the resonant objective domains.
- *Instruments:* Be specific and provide samples of evaluation instruments such as tests, quizzes, or any other method you may employ.
- *Grading:* Provide detailed information about the grading system you are going to use. Is it pass/no credit, letter grade, or audit?

Participant Prerequisites

This key element of creditworthiness should provide the framework surrounding a participant's involvement in a course, including his or her qualifications to enroll and participate. Detailed standards should exist for participation including technical, professional, and educational thresholds.

Facilitator Prerequisites

Always make sure you have provided detailed specifications for those who will be teaching your course, including

- *Qualification:* Are there detailed thresholds for facilitation, including education level, certification, experience, relationship to organization and content?
- *Documentation:* For documenting qualifications of facilitators, present a plan that fits into the organizational structure of the sponsoring institution.

Deliverables

Nothing too complicated here, just be thorough. Provide a list of all the deliverables from the course design process including the design plan, lesson plan, materials, evaluation instruments, and everything else listed in the design plan as a tangible element of the course.

In Conclusion

This chapter identified some of the major design elements to consider if you are interested in pursuing credit options for a course design. It is important to remember that even if a course is designed to be eligible for credit, numerous factors including, but not limited to, specific rules and regulations govern the process and creditworthiness is not in any way a certainty for any course. Since this chapter presents some general guidelines to consider in the process, and does not represent any specific institution or situation, you must always take the time to find out what is required in each individual training and education environment and work from those guidelines as you design.

Putting What You Have Learned Into Action

Reviewing design plan data for suitability in a for-credit environment begins with the notion that there needs to be a link between the needs of an accrediting body or partner and the design of a course. Although this process is different for each particular situation, having some basic points of review, as offered in exercise 14-1 on the CD, will help you get started.

Section 5 Tips for Success

15 Fine-Tuning Your Skills

Chapter Objectives

At the conclusion of this chapter, you should be able to describe the significance of each of the following instructional designer's tools:

- mental strategies
- avoidance of role conflict
- jargon control
- designer neutrality
- knowledge of designer types
- ability to deal with failure
- thinking big
- value-neutral design.

Advancing Your Skills

Once instructional designers become comfortable with instructional design as a profession, they often quickly rise within the ranks of an organization based on the variety of adjunct skills they bring to the table, not solely their instructional design skills. These same skills enable some designers to start their own design firms and manage both a design process and a business venture. Others rise through the faculty ranks at academic institutions and often accept positions managing curriculum development and designers.

Designers are systems analysts at heart, and the skills required for this type of professional rigor often spill into related skill sets, including project management and leadership. It is for this reason that instructional designers at any career stage should expand their view over the immediate horizon of instructional design and see what other opportunities present themselves. The list of considerations that follows provides a starting point for this discussion, and as such it would serve every designer to scan the immediate environment for opportunities that lend themselves to designer-based skills and professional practice.

Why Learn These Tools?

Once a designer has learned to create a design plan and lesson plan, he or she knows most of what it takes to prepare and present a really great instructional package. However, being a great instructional designer involves knowing some of the rules of the road about working in the profession. These tools help designers go further in their careers by filling in some of the gaps between preparing and presenting an instructional package and working in the profession.

Mental Strategies

One of the most valuable skills any professional develops is the ability to master the *mental strategies* necessary for the profession. It is the silent churning of the brain that calls forward every relevant bit of data relating to a situation. Some call it the sixth sense, others, second nature. Whatever its name, this background of information professionals have about their specific profession sets them apart from everyone else. It develops from both experience and formal instruction.

Police officers realize that one of the most valuable elements of that profession is the sixth sense they acquire about their surroundings after years of experience. That sense is vitally important and actually saves lives in certain situations.

Professionals in any field approach problems differently than the untrained. This is exactly what happens in every facet of life. The tow truck driver changes your tire in the time it would take you to open the trunk. A heating and air conditioning technician pushes one button and resets the fuse on the nonfunctioning heat pump that has been off for the last three cold nights.

Designers gain experience by working in the field with other professionals just as professionals do in any other occupation. Some fortunate new designers are lucky enough to have mentors to guide them along. Even those who do not get that guidance can find ample opportunities to keep themselves sharp. The apprenticeship approach for designers usually encompasses watching, working, and waiting. The watching and working aspects are obvious, but the waiting may not be. Unless a designer is fortunate enough to work in an organization that is constantly providing opportunities for learning, designers in training spend most of their time waiting—waiting for something new to do or waiting for a new design challenge besides new employee orientation.

This waiting period proves most frustrating for new designers and may dull the design senses, but this is a prime time for them to focus on important mental strategies by thinking about them and reviewing them in books and articles. As designers develop a toolkit full of these strategies, they can add to their skills regardless of the opportunities for experiential growth.

An example of a mental strategy is the way a designer determines if a performance problem has a training solution. Billions of dollars are wasted each year trying to remedy problems that cannot be fixed with training solutions. How often will time-management training be used to solve the problem of poor working conditions or a terrible boss? Don't forget the cardinal rule of analysis from chapter 2: Make sure you have a training issue to solve before you provide a training solution.

Another example is designers' focus on objectives, not just on developing goals. A goal for a training course might be improving productivity. An objective might be that the participant should be able to complete all necessary company paperwork without error. See the difference? Goals point you in the right direction, whereas objectives get you there.

Role Conflict

The issue of *role conflict* is a constant in the life of an instructional designer. For example, instructional designers spend much time attempting to point out to SMEs how much they can contribute to making a project work. It is sometimes difficult for nondesigners to accept that expertise in a content area does not directly correlate with curriculum design expertise.

Some of the hardest work for designers is convincing SMEs that they are better off leaving instructional design to the designers. Some would argue that this do-it-all attitude is more pronounced among SMEs in academics than in other professional fields. It is, nonetheless, a real issue for discussion in any training project.

The realization that they can't do it all requires the same mental process that most people go through when they try to fix a plumbing problem. Plumbers say their best service calls are from clients who have first tried to fix stopped-up sinks themselves. When a do-it-yourself plumber finally makes the call to a professional one, the problem is often worse than it was before the amateurs went to work. The plumbers make twice as much money as they would have had they been called at the first sign of trouble, and the homeowner is happy to pay every penny of it. Similarly, when people with no ISD background try to design training programs, their results are unworkable, and they usually end up calling in the training experts.

It may be necessary for designers to have several run-ins with SMEs or their managers before they earn their respect and acceptance as part of the team. They should never take it personally if people question or challenge the value added by the ISD process. Every designer hears these questions. For each project, designers should develop a list of contributions that they will make. This list will help clarify responsibilities and will minimize the likelihood for misunderstandings later. Eventually the issue of role conflict becomes just one more part of the process and is managed easily.

Jargon Control

Have you ever wondered why professionals feel the need to impress everyone with their ability to use big words and profession-related *jargon*? There should be a study to document every word, acronym, or unintelligible bit of jargon used with the intent to impress or intimidate. Just think back to the last time you were subjected to jargon speak, and you can understand how destructive it can be to the communications process unless everyone uses the same language. Can anyone explain why lawyers say "pro bono" instead of the word "free"?

Jargon, like the nine events of instruction or performance agreement, is an important concept in the instructional design profession. Certain terminology is so common to designers that they are apt to use it without being aware that it is special to the field. It is best not to use these terms with anyone not trained in ISD, including managers, clients, and the audience, at any function where the designer is the guest speaker. In short, designers must be careful to use professional jargon only when necessary and never outside the ISD family.

Designer Neutrality

Designer neutrality relates directly to issues of a political nature within an office. Numerous situations will arise in which someone tries to force a curriculum designer to express an opinion in an area not related to design. These occurrences are most common when the clients are predominately internal. The office wars and personality conflicts that besiege every organization are not fertile grounds for designers. In other words, designers should not get involved in nondesign issues outside of their office.

Neutrality directly relates to credibility. Designers may never get the respect of their client group if they wander too far away from designing. Designers who express an opinion about anything outside the sphere of the project may suggest to clients that they have a personal agenda.

Subject matter is an especially dangerous area for designers to meddle with. A designer can ruin a focus group or client meeting by expressing an opinion about a topic. Suppose a designer is in the middle of a meeting with an internal client on a proposed hot-topic course. Several times the designer has commented on the subject matter in a way that suggests he or she has an opinion. The designer may later have to defend the design because someone thinks the content slants toward the designer's views. Right or wrong, the designer is now part of the problem, and the designer's solutions may lack credibility no matter how well designed the training is.

Designers who are external to an organization really can get dragged through the mud. People involved in office warfare love to have validation, and someone from the outside agreeing with them is usually all it takes to get something started. Just as with the internal client situations, designers should stick to design issues and avoid getting in the middle of office wars.

Types of Designers

Instructional designers can get involved in ISD in a number of different ways. It seems that almost every facet of training can take advantage of the benefits offered by this process. No matter which role a designer is in now, there are probably a large number of people in the same position. Here are several of the roles that designers might play:

- ■ *Designer and manager:* In this role, a designer also has the responsibility for managing all or a portion of a project or projects.
- ■ *Full-time ISD manager:* An ISD manager does little or no design work and manages one or more projects.
- ■ *Full-time designer:* This person does nothing but instructional design.
- ■ *Designer and facilitator:* This individual both designs the course and is the facilitator.
- ■ *Training staff:* This group of training professionals does everything from design to facilitation.
- ■ *Freelance consultant and designer:* This independent contractor works for a number of different employers.
- ■ *Specialist in one or more ISD elements:* This designer concentrates on one element of the ADDIE model, usually analysis or evaluation.

All of these roles, and many more, represent the varied situations in which designers might find themselves at any given point in their career. There are several reasons it is important to consider the different contexts in which instructional designers may work. First, novice designers should have a good grasp of the different possibilities they may face in the field. Second, there is no one right or wrong way to work as an instructional designer. One way is no purer than another. Third, instructional designers should consider the best fit for a combination of skills and other factors related to job satisfaction. Some may be happier working alone in a small organization than working in a team in a larger setting.

Designers and Failure

Anyone can have a bad day when he or she is prone to mistakes. Designers are no different. If someone tried to write down every mistake he or she has made as a designer, it would challenge this book in length. Although it may seem unnecessary to mention this in an otherwise upbeat book, it warrants discussion.

Police cadets are often taught that the most dangerous times for police officers are their first six months on the job and the last six months before retirement. New officers don't have the experience to always know what to do, and experienced officers have survived a long time and think nothing new can happen to them. Similarly, new designers have a greater probability of making mistakes because they lack experience. When they have been a designer for a while, they tend to become complacent and careless.

Recently, an experienced designer was participating in several focus groups with high-school students that their teachers attended as observers. This group was a little different from the usual population of adults with which the designer worked. Forgetting that teachers like to teach, the designer sat in horror as a teacher got up and taught the students a lesson on the topic during the focus group.

That was a bad day for the veteran designer, but the designer did leave with some very important lessons: Make sure you have a plan and that everyone is clear on the process and always follows the plan.

Sounds simple, but focus groups can get out of control and it takes a good facilitator to make them work the way they should. When those bad days come, it is good to remember that everyone goofs or gets complacent now and then.

Thinking Big

One tool that a designer needs to perfect is the practice of *universality*. To a designer that means designing as if his or her curriculum will be implemented in a thousand places at once by a thousand different facilitators. Another aspect of this concept is the notion that the designer will never see, meet, or come in contact with anyone that takes a course he or she has designed.

This tool is important even if a designer plans to implement the course with a group of participants with whom he or she is familiar. It enables great designers to look outside their safety zone and review every aspect of a project as if the safety net of familiarity were removed.

This second aspect gets us to a very important issue with designers, separating design work from facilitating. Although some designers do actually play both the designer and facilitator roles, they should design the curriculum as if they will never play both roles.

A friend once commented to me that one of the more serious issues in the training environment was the great teacher complex. This malady usually affects facilitators who think they can just stand in front of a group of learners and impart wisdom by the barrelful.

Designers need to be cognizant of the great teacher traits in all of us. This malady will keep designers from preparing the kind of design that any facilitator can use. Instead, they will prepare a design for their own use on the assumption that they can handle any situation that might occur while they are facilitating a course. These designers may not consider a wide array of problems as they prepare their plans, including learners who ask questions far off topic, whether the lesson will run short or long, and whether there is too much or too little content at an inappropriate level for the population. Their disregard for these fundamental concerns is acceptable if no one else will ever use the designs, but that is not always the case. In fact, many designers never actually facilitate their designs.

An important tool in a designer's repertoire is the ability to wear only one hat at a time: either designer or facilitator. Never try to wear both at the same time. Confusion can occur when designers tend to rely on their facilitation skills and subject matter knowledge, as opposed to analysis data, as the following example shows. An instructional designer with a computer science background has the responsibility to design and facilitate a course for a common software package. The analysis shows that the facilitators are from within the organization and are good at using computers, but have no background in computer science. For the course, the basis of the training is the designer's subject matter and facilitation skills. Although the designer includes key concepts in the lesson plan, there is very little detailed information about the workings of the program. The designer would have been able to provide that information in class, but the facilitators cannot fill in the blanks missing in the lesson plan. The course flops because the facilitators cannot provide the missing information, and the designer who has the knowledge is not the facilitator.

Every designer should use personal facilitation skills as one component of good design practice but avoid the trap of leaving out key information or instructions based on one's personal ability to facilitate a particular course. It is a much better practice to put too much detail into a course instead of too little. Facilitators can always select from the information offered.

The Value-Neutral Designer

All of us have opinions. These opinions are based on any number of experiences, cultural and environmental influences, and sometimes even the magazines that greet us in the checkout line at the grocery. Although designers' biases travel with them as they carry out instructional design, it is important always to maintain a professional distance, or *value neutrality,* from these issues. The only opinions reflected in instructional design should be those related to curriculum development, and the closer a designer can stick to that philosophy the more likely it is that a project will avoid the pitfalls of polarization within a workgroup.

The description of focus groups in chapter 2 mentioned the importance of neutrality while facilitating or designing these types of analysis vehicles. The same must be true of the entire process of designing curricula. If a designer wanders at all from the center of the road, focus might be lost.

The designer's tool of neutrality is not a natural instinct for most of us. Most of us must at times exercise a great deal of conscious effort to keep our personal, non-professional opinions to ourselves. Some designers may rightly argue that opinions are the very energy that drove them to be a designer in the first place; and that is a legitimate motivation. Nevertheless, it is important to remember that noninstructional opinions are usually best left out of the process of instructional design.

Designers work in every conceivable type of environment, from the desert heat of Egypt to the top floor of a multinational corporation. Neutrality relates to process and content and in no way negates loyalty to the organization. A designer should stay out of the opinion business except pertaining to design issues.

The following example will show what happens when neutrality is not maintained during the design process. An organization has requested a course on a controversial subject, perhaps sexual misconduct in the workplace. This topic attracts polarizing opinions and has tainted the workplace culture. As the designer visits the cafeteria for refills of hours-old coffee, employees ask about the design department's views of the subject. If the designer expresses an opinion, the credibility of the design work diminishes, negating the value of the designer's efforts, no matter what opinion the designer expresses.

In Conclusion

In this chapter, the role of an instructional designer is seen in a different context. The more subtle art of working as a project manager, facilitator, and leader is highlighted. Even the most seasoned designer can profit from a review of the topics in this chapter.

Putting What You Have Learned Into Action

Exercises 15-1 to 15-8 on the CD offer you the opportunity to fine-tune your own skills.

16 Working Solo as a Designer

Chapter Objectives

At the conclusion of this chapter, you should be able to

- identify several roles that the solo designer will have to fill
- construct at least three strategies to assist you when working as a solo designer.

On Your Own as a Designer

There are as many environments in which instructional designers might find themselves as there are designers. One of the realities of instructional design is the fact that designers often find themselves working as a committee of one in the design process, being a SME, material development specialist, project manager, and every other role possible in the design process. Additionally, a designer may even have to implement his or her own designs.

Because every design project is, by its nature, meant to be implemented in a population that does not include the designer, receiving feedback and input is critical in this design space. This entails more than the expected interaction between client and designer (assuming there is a client) because this is usually not a designer-to-designer relationship. What is needed is a process to assure yourself that your design is both viable and sound as reflected by the review of other designers.

> Working solo is not necessarily a bad thing; in fact, many designers work in this environment, even in large organizations. They may only work collaboratively at certain critical points as a project matures. My informal research shows that many instructional designers are introverts and, as such, feel as comfortable—or more comfortable—working on their own as they do in a group setting.

There are several very important process issues to consider if you find yourself in this position. Although not all of the strategies discussed in this chapter will apply to your situation, it is important that you consider the usefulness of each of these suggestions.

Isolate Roles

Simply stated, when in the design process, think and act as an instructional designer. This may seem painfully obvious in theory, but it is much more difficult to achieve in practice because role conflict can potentially influence your design decisions and your final product. Remember that an instructional designer is the project manager in this process. Discussion and arbitration of differing views and perspectives are a natural part of the design process; if a designer working solo ignores alternative possibilities, or fails to conduct a 360-degree scan of the design environment, the final product may suffer.

At this point, you might be saying to yourself, "But, I'm working alone. What does this have to do with my situation?" The answer is everything. Having tunnel vision is an occupational hazard in this environment. Allowing yourself the luxury of segmenting your responsibilities makes you more efficient and productive. Let's look at several important aspects of this challenge and what you can do to make it work for you.

Designer Before Facilitator

The most common example of this role conflict is the very different roles of designer and facilitator/teacher. While in the design process, always make decisions based on your role as an instructional designer rather than as the implementer of the final product. This doesn't mean you ignore your experience in the classroom or online, it means you integrate your experience into your design. In other words, consult your teacher-self about issues that relate to that area of your experience.

Experience shows that course designs that reflect choices made mainly from the perspective of a teacher are generally less detailed, less well documented, and less likely to contain alternative strategies for issues that might be encountered in implementation than would choices made from the perspective of a designer. The reasons behind this phenomenon are numerous, but the most obvious is that seasoned facilitators can manage most challenges during implementation. Brevity of design reflects internal confidence that might not be justified. This perspective is especially damaging for designers who will not be implementing a course they design.

Leave the Nest for Review and Evaluation

One of the most challenging aspects of working alone is catching less-than-obvious errors and refining the tough elements of your designs. We have all had the experience of having a simple spelling or grammatical error grow wings and take on a life of its own. Working briefly with another solo designer as you write objectives and lesson plans can help you catch errors and identify gaps in these critical elements of your design.

The Rule of a Thousand

You will find it exponentially useful to think of your design projects as having a life that is beyond your control. For this purpose, the rule of a thousand makes this point exceptionally well. Try thinking about your role as the designer in this context: Imagine every course you design will be implemented in 1,000 places at once, by 1,000 facilitators, in front of 1,000 populations you will never meet. As frightening as this may seem, it can help focus your work as a designer.

The rule of a thousand also helps to clear away role conflict issues associated with a designer designing as a facilitator. This is not to say that your skills in facilitation are wasted or of no consequence; in fact, quite the opposite is true. You must isolate your design and facilitation skills while incorporating your specific experience in implementation in your design process. Nevertheless, as you design, keep in mind that you won't be able to rely on your own abilities as a facilitator to rush in to save a course or make changes on the fly to correct problems.

Ideas to Consider

Here are several ways to mitigate the solo designer syndrome:

- Find at least one trading partner who will review your work in exchange for the same from you. Make sure this is an instructional designer at your level of experience or higher, or you may become frustrated with the process. If you can build a group of designers that meets regularly to talk about projects, this is also very useful. ASTD meetings are a perfect place to find other designers interested in the same support.

169

- Create templates for key design elements so that the process takes a back seat to the product and you can spend your valuable creativity on your design.
- Where practical, let every element of your design sit for at least a day. Problems and solutions almost jump off the screen toward you after a short mental break.
- Don't reach beyond your limitations. Ask for help. Don't be afraid to send an email or call a trusted designer and ask for an opinion.
- Don't spend your time on tasks that can be more efficiently performed by someone else. If something is truly more work than it is worth, find a way to outsource it and build it into the bid next time you have a similar situation. Don't pretend you can do it all.
- Read your copy backward from the end to the beginning. You will be surprised how many errors you can detect this way.
- Always take advantage of the technology and use the spelling and grammar checking options in your word-processing software. This seems so obvious, but it is often ignored in the fog of a deadline.
- Back up your work. Because you probably don't have a network and systemwide backup capacity, make sure you have a routine for saving your files either in a fireproof safe or off site in a bank's safety deposit box. Unfortunately, you will probably ignore this advice until you learn the hard way how important this is.

In Conclusion

This chapter outlined strategies to consider when working as a solo designer.

Putting What You Have Learned Into Action

Exercise 16-1 on the CD gives you a chance to plan strategies to address the challenges that exist when working solo as a designer. Feel free to expand this exercise to include items that have not been addressed in this chapter but are challenges in your design environment.

17 Distance Learning and Design Sense

Chapter Objectives

At the conclusion of this chapter, you should be able to

- identify several distance learning components you can integrate into your designs
- list at least three design issues related to distance learning.

The concept of distance learning has been around for at least 300 years, perhaps longer depending on how you define the term. From the earliest forms of correspondence learning to the latest online course management tools, distance learning is a valuable asset to an instructional designer. It is important to remember that distance learning, from an instructional design perspective, is just one of many settings for training and education. After all, instructional design, at its core, is only a system. Any implementation modality, including distance learning, is simply one aspect of your design system.

Arriving at a design decision to use distance learning, classroom learning, or some combination requires a design process that involves the advantages and disadvantages of each option available. It is exactly the same decision-making process as needing to travel to a city across the country and deciding which form of transportation to use for your trip. You will make the best decision in either of these cases if you weigh a number of important factors including cost, convenience, and access. Taking a hot air balloon from Baltimore to Los Angeles might seem attractive until you step into the basket and realize there is more to the trip than just a great view.

There are as many variations on distance learning as there are instructional designers and learners. Implementation does not have to be all or nothing with distance learning; it can also effectively be adjunct to the core instructional methodology by utilizing message boards, online assignment posting, resources availability, synchronous chat rooms, and hundreds of combinations of these and other methods.

Glamorizing distance learning into something more than it is—an implementation method—increases the likelihood that the technology will be selected solely for the iconic value of the technology itself. Distance learning can be very seductive, and falling blindly for a vendor's promises could leave even an accomplished designer with major, unexpected challenges. Just because a learner has access to the Internet and an organization has a network server and a webpage does not mean that distance learning is the best design choice. The seasoned instructional designer harmonizes all aspects of the population, budget, resources, content, objective domains, and performance agreement when deciding how to implement a learning program.

Design Issues

Important instructional design decisions for distance learning can usually be reduced to essentially the same questions a designer should ask about any implementation choices. However, it is necessary to expand the complexity of the discussion with distance learning to the degree that questions need to be answered in several key areas.

In this chapter, *distance learning,* or e-learning, refers to some form of online learning requiring that a learner have both a computer and network access (Internet, intranet, dial-up, and so forth). It is beyond the scope of this discussion to go into the different hardware, software, course management tools, and other very specific details of online learning. There are excellent sources for that information. The important thing to remember is that these specifics will always be changing and what is hot today will be a dinosaur tomorrow. It is the job of a great instructional designer to keep current with the technology while never losing sight of the ISD process. In the end, because instructional design is sufficiently dynamic to allow for implementation of any future technologies, such technologies become just another variable in the design equation.

Population

Any distance learning discussion needs to start with the population it is meant to serve. You must determine if your target population is suited for distance learning and has a reasonable chance for success in that environment. All other decisions rest on this decision. Keep these factors in mind when evaluating the target population:

- *Access to technology:* The digital divide is real and becomes more of an issue with each new generation of hardware and software. Dial-up and the newest advances in fiber-optic broadband access are miles distant in terms of speed, much the same as walking compared to taking a plane to a distant destination. Although you can be creative with how you package online content and supplement with digital media such as DVDs and CDs, there are limits on the end learner that you must honor.

- *Learning styles:* Are your learners predominantly visual or auditory learners? Or, like most populations, are your learners a combination of several styles? Are they well suited to learn online? Are they comfortable with online requirements such as reading online content and posting comments?

- *Learning environment:* There are learners who prefer online to classroom instruction, and others who prefer classroom to online. Although the reasons for these preferences vary among learners, in some cases, a blended approach combining aspects of both can accommodate the needs of all types of learners.

- *Timing:* If you are going to require synchronous activities (everyone online at the same time), can your population meet at the assigned times? Ten in the evening in New York City is noon in Seoul, South Korea.

- *Technical competence:* Are learners able to use the technology to the degree required for successful participation? Everything from keyboarding skills to working around access issues, such as firewalls and different operating systems, can create frustration and impact completion rates.

Cost

The cost of distance learning in today's design environment can range from negligible to enormous depending on the requirements of a design. A college or university hosting a course management system for distance learning can quickly get to six figures just to get up and running. On the other hand, there are low-cost solutions if you want to dig around and find a product that meets your design requirements. There are several things to keep in mind:

- *Expectations:* Learners have become just as sophisticated as the technologies now available. If a distance learning course is perceived as dated because of its interface or usability, learners may be disappointed or end up being frustrated while they participate.

- *Production values:* Developing high-end distance learning generally requires expensive resources because such features as animation, audio, video, and editing may be required. Think of the difference in production quality between the average cable-access television program and a high-def network-produced show. For a more direct example, compare the average user-developed website with the online products from a major Internet organization. Learners will make the comparisons, and your population profile will tell you whether this is an issue for you to consider.

■ *Media:* If you are going to incorporate audio or video components into your distance learning design, you need to be prepared for the costs associated with this design choice. Yes, you could use a $50 webcam and microphone, but would the resulting quality meet your client's or your population's expectations for a course?

Content

Certain content areas drive a decision concerning online learning suitability. Here are a couple of things to consider:

■ *Objective domains:* Is your content in a domain that requires hands-on or first-person demonstration, either for presentation or evaluation? If so, can you meet this design need using distance learning?

■ *Transposition of content:* Will you need to transpose content from one format to another, for example, handouts and other materials to online accessibility? Can this transposition be accomplished easily and inexpensively?

Evaluation

This can sometimes be a very complicated area of online learning. Keep these issues in mind:

■ *Formal evaluation:* If you are required to have formal evaluations for a course, will you be able to provide an accepted environment for that process? Many for-credit and ACE requirements demand that you provide a proctored test environment for online courses. Make sure you know what is required in your content and accreditation environment early in the design process so that you do not have any surprises later. Finding proctors for a national program is not a small logistical or budgetary issue.

■ *Performance agreement:* Can you evaluate your objectives in the same domain in which they are written? For example, if your objectives are in the psychomotor domain, will you be able to evaluate in that domain?

Implementation

When implementing your lesson plan, consider these aspects of the design:

- *Facilitator workload:* It generally takes more time to facilitate an online course than a similar classroom-based course. Although this can be mitigated by design choices, it is still something to keep in mind.
- *Synchronous or asynchronous:* If you are going to incorporate synchronous activities, make sure your technology is learner-friendly. Many chat-room environments in course-management software leave much to be desired, and these have a way of diverging into off-topic chats unless they are closely facilitated.
- *User satisfaction:* Does the implementation mode match the needs of the learner? Is it the best choice?

In Conclusion

Convenience is a common motivation for adults who choose to participate in distance learning. All things being equal, this is a reasonable learner expectation. From the delivery side of the distance learning equation, increasing participation, cost, and access are important considerations. It is up to the designer to see that the experience is of equal or better quality than the same content delivered in any other format. It is the designer's obligation to detail the challenges that each choice offers and weigh the advantages and disadvantages of each. At least everyone will be working with the same data for making decisions.

Putting What You Have Learned Into Action

Now it's time to take the concepts involved in distance learning and relate them to a specific design project. Try your hand at exercise 17-1 on the CD.

18 Wrapping It Up

Practicing as an instructional designer can reveal a dizzying variety of challenges in a constantly changing training and education environment. It sometimes seems as though the practice of ISD changes on a daily basis. Sometimes the focus is on distance learning, sometimes on performance improvement, at other times the focus is on nothing at all and leaves designers wondering what the next wave of ISD issues will involve.

The truth of ISD and the practice of instructional design is that the basics will always remain the same within the profession. Distance learning and performance improvement are simply new wrinkles in a system that at its heart is based on the very simple concept of the ADDIE model and the importance of using a systems approach when working as an instructional designer. The answers in instructional design are as varied as the questions, and anyone who thinks ISD is about predetermined answers or outcomes simply misses the point. ISD is about process, and the product that follows is the result of that effort.

As such, there isn't a single element of instructional design that is too difficult to learn or use. As with any other professional pursuit, mastering a basic set of skills and learning the tricks of the trade bring it all together. The process of designing training may appear easy and uncomplicated to people outside the process. After all, well-designed training does appear seamless and almost effortless to the observer as it is being implemented. That is one of the ironies of instructional design: The better the course goes, the less chance there is that anyone will appreciate the effort that went into it.

Designers who use the design and lesson plan approach presented in this book have the opportunity to combine a number of ISD skills and, consequently, to construct almost any training project that makes its way to their door.

Most designers incorporate elements of a design plan or a lesson plan in their work although they may never have known what each separate element is called or even its full value. For example, a designer may have incorporated a course rationale into a verbal presentation to a client without understanding why it made a difference to the course, or a designer may have written facilitator prerequisites without studying why they matter in the project. In the case of lesson plans, many designers use some type of format, but may have never realized that there was a sequence that supports the way a participant learns and retains information. Without a complete understanding of the elements of the design and lesson plans, designers may not take the necessary steps consistently and may not follow through with them in a way that will benefit the learners.

Designers' jobs are easier when they see ISD as a process and apply names to the different elements. Their good instincts about how best to design a project, combined with a systems approach to training and education, provide a solid foundation for design.

Following is an overview of this book's systems approach to developing training. ISD is represented by a number of well-thought-out models, but designers most commonly use the ADDIE model. Designers should work toward developing their own ISD model based on their experience and support systems including this book. Most designers end up doing that anyway, although most are unaware of what they have created.

Reviewing the ADDIE Model

A summary of each of the five elements in the ADDIE model of ISD follows.

Analysis

During the analysis phase of ISD, a designer needs to make sure that every atom of data is collected. Designers need to be data magnets and attract everything of value into the design process. They must

- ask every question and not move on without an answer
- fill boxes full of results from web searches or other data if necessary
- conduct focus groups or undertake other data-gathering methods as necessary.

When they have gathered all the data, designers need to ask four questions:

1. *How will learners be different after the training?* Will they have a new skill, knowledge, or ability, such as enhanced language capabilities or a better way to process anger in the workplace? Designers should always determine the objectives.

2. *How will learners meet the objectives?* Have the distribution and instructional methods been selected? The choices are endless, but designers must decide methods early in the process to eliminate wasted time and energy later.

3. *How will designers know when the learners have met the objectives?* Have designers decided which of the evaluation methods are appropriate for their objectives and methods? Designers should prepare evaluations at the same time that they write the objectives.

4. *How does the sponsor of the training define success?* If the sponsor's expectations are unknown, there is little chance of ever making him or her happy. It is almost impossible to hit a moving target. Designers have to ask until they get an answer.

Design

Design is the unique element of ISD, with no professional equivalent in other fields. It is here that the project gets a designer's touch. Designers prepare the objectives and evaluation tasks, writing, rewriting, and writing again until they work. They choose the distribution and instructional methods and prepare drafts of materials and media. During design, the data gathered in analysis evolves into the clarity and purpose that a project needs to be successful. A design plan becomes the blueprint for the rest of a project.

Development

Development is pasting the project together. Sometimes designers do it all and develop their own materials and media. Other times they are responsible for managing the process. It can be challenging to work with computer programmers, graphic artists, compositors, video producers, and printers, but it is also satisfying to see ideas become great materials, ready for final production after pilot testing.

Pilot testing ensures that a project is ready for the big time before it moves to implementation. Actors rehearse their lines before a play opens, and musicians practice for hours to perfect a melody before an audience hears a note. In similar fashion, designers use pilot tests to give training an opportunity to muff its lines or hit a wrong note before learners have an opportunity to take a course.

Designers shouldn't get discouraged if they end up doing the design and development work without any help. Multimedia CDs, four-color manuals, and videos with high production values are the exception to the rule for training design. Most organizations can't afford to implement every project on the Internet or have materials that have the appearance of a coffee table book. The resources and funding for design work are still largely limited.

Implementation

Implementation usually finds designers in front of the learners or in back of them. Designers may be facilitating, evaluating, or both. Until people outside of the process of ISD acquire an appreciation of all the work that goes into it, they are not likely to be aware of any ISD element but implementation. However, designers know that implementation is the ISD equivalent of hanging a newly completed painting. The work is now ready for appreciation.

Designers make sure that the evaluation plan is in effect and that all of the information from the evaluation process is gathered. The facilitator may make necessary changes in the training on the fly during implementation, or the designer will make them later, as the dust settles.

Evaluation

Evaluation, the fifth element in the ADDIE model, is always looking over a designer's shoulders. Just as 3-year-old children believe that Santa knows if they have been good or bad, evaluation always knows whether training has met the mark. Santa and evaluation share the same quality of vigilance. The difference between good training and bad training is listening to what evaluation has to say. This is very hard to do if a designer does not allow evaluation to be a major component of the design process.

Kirkpatrick (1998) has given designers a brilliant framework for evaluation: four different boxes into which most evaluation needs fit. A designer may want to use two, three, or all of these levels of evaluation, depending on the needs.

Level 1 evaluations are based on learners' reactions to training. Did they like it? Did they find it worth their investment of time? Did the distribution and instructional methods find favor with the learners? Were the bagels fresh and the coffee hot? These are all reactions to the training, every single moment of it.

Level 2 evaluations are the same as the evaluations written for objectives. Designers are measuring each learner's ability to meet an objective. Designers must always be sure that the learner is meeting objectives.

Level 3 evaluations are the way to determine if the training made any difference in a learner's ability to meet the objectives. It is not unusual for evaluations to be performed three, six, or even 12 months after the training. This information allows a designer to compare results and determine the staying power of the training.

Level 4 evaluations measure the business-level impact of ROI of a project. Although usually best left to the accountants because of the financial nature of the process, level 4 evaluation has a place in most projects, and designers should not ignore the long-term value that it brings. Large corporations can calculate business impact in the millions of dollars; a community group can figure the bottom-line impact by the number of new adult readers who can perform a valuable skill. Either way, designers' work has value, and they should think about the impact the training may have on the learner or sponsor.

Accumulation of Advantages

The introduction to this book mentioned the term *accumulation of advantages.* It is the process of performing a number of separate design skills that meld together to become a finished design project. All of the ADDIE elements need to be present for an accumulation of advantages to exist. Doing less than five phases, such as eliminating analysis and evaluation, offers little hope for a successful training project. Accumulate all of the advantages offered by utilizing ISD and reap the benefits of well-conceived and delivered training.

Rechecking Your Skills

Now that you have completed all of the chapters, you can evaluate how your ending skills compare with those when you began this book. This is a pre/post evaluation of your progress. Look through the list in table 18-1 and answer the questions "yes" or "no." When you are done, compare your answers to the skills inventory you completed in the Introduction (table I-1). How did you do? If you are still uncertain about any of these instructional design elements, review the chapter associated with the skill.

Table 18-1. Ending skills inventory.

Do You Know How to...	Yes	No
Conduct a population analysis?	☐	☐
Design and implement a focus group session?	☐	☐
Write four-part objectives?	☐	☐
Name the four objective domains?	☐	☐
Define and provide examples of at least three instructional methods?	☐	☐
Define and provide examples of at least three distribution methods?	☐	☐
Write at least two evaluation tasks?	☐	☐
Explain the performance agreement principle using an example?	☐	☐
Design evaluations for each of the four Kirkpatrick levels?	☐	☐
Complete a design plan?	☐	☐
Construct a lesson plan?	☐	☐

The Power of ISD

The real power of ISD lies in its ability to provide a foundation for the instructional design process. The work that builds on this foundation can have numerous variations to fit designers' changing needs. The system itself is endlessly evolving within the mind and imagination of each separate designer. This process is only as rigid as a designer wants it to be.

Feel free to play a dominant role in the evolution of the ISD process by revising the ideas in this book to fit your particular needs. With the new skills now in your inventory, you should be ready to meet any design challenge.

References

Bassi, L.J., and M.E. Van Buren. (1999). *ASTD State of the Industry Report.* Alexandria, VA: ASTD Press.

Gagne, R.M., L.J. Briggs, and W.W. Wager. (1988). *Principles of Instructional Design* (3rd edition). New York: Holt, Rinehart & Winston.

Johnson, J., Robinson, J., and Welch, S. (2004). *Pocket Guide to College Credits and Degrees: Valuable Information for Adult Learners.* Washington, D.C.: American Council on Education.

Kirkpatrick, D. (1998). *Evaluating Training Programs: The Four Levels* (2nd edition). San Francisco: Berrett-Koehler.

Romiszowski, A.J. (1981). "The How and Why of Performance Objectives." In: *Designing Instructional Systems.* New York and London: Kogan Page Limited/Nichols Publishing Company.

About the Author

Chuck Hodell is associate director of the University of Maryland Baltimore County (UMBC) graduate program in ISD. He is also deputy provost of the National Labor College in Silver Spring, Maryland. He has published numerous articles on instructional design for ASTD. He has a doctoral degree in language, literacy, and culture from UMBC, where he also received his master's degree in instructional design. His undergraduate degree is from Antioch University—the George Meany Center for Labor Studies. He resides on Kent Island on Maryland's Eastern Shore. You may contact him by email at hodell@umbc.edu.

Index